JOY-WORTHY:

A mother's guide to more joy, less stress and no guilt

JULIE McGRATH

founder of The Joy Source

Published by
The Joy Source, LLC
P.O. Box 3243
Peabody, MA 01960

Quantity sales: For information on bulk purchases, please contact The Joy Source, LLC.

First Edition November 2012
Editor: Kate Victory Hannisian, Blue Pencil Consulting
Book and Cover Design: Lisa McKenna, Curious Marie LLC
Printing: King Printing Co., Inc.
Cover photograph: FWStudio/Shutterstock.com

ISBN: 978-0-9884788-0-0

DEDICATION AND HEARTFELT THANKS:

....

To my parents, who taught me how to live a life of celebration, joy and purpose.

To all my friends who inspire me to be my best, thank you.

To Elisa, my true friend and confidante, whose words of guidance and
encouragement have kept me afloat.

To the love of my life, with you by my side, all is possible.

This book is dedicated to all the mothers out there who are giving it their all each
and every day, may you always feel worthy of unlimited JOY.

Praise for *Joy-Worthy*

"Just surviving motherhood is not enough—it is time for women to start living a joy-driven life. Laundry, kids, work, husbands/partners—the challenges of motherhood haven't changed, but women have. Julie doesn't just lead the charge with her wit, experience and interactive exercises; she is living proof that joy is waiting for any mother who is willing to seek it. This book should be on the nightstand of every woman who has children, is having children or has ever thought about having children."

–SHANNON DANFORD, AUTHOR OF *FREEZER BURN BLUES* AND *BRIDGE CLUB BLUES*
(AND YOGA INSTRUCTOR WHO BELIEVES IN JULIE'S MESSAGE)

"Calling all mommies! Calling all mommies! It's finally here! A down-to-earth self-help book about motherhood that keeps it real. Run, don't walk, to get your very own copy!"

–FOUNDER OF THE BLOG, WHERE'S THE F*#KING MOMMY MANUAL?
WWW.WHERESTHEFCKINGMOMMYMANUAL.WORDPRESS.COM

"As a mom of three, I've found this book has helped me to realize that I'm not alone in my feelings of being overwhelmed and tired. Joy-Worthy offers great tips and advice on how to regain the 'me' I lost in the chaos of becoming a wife and mom. I'm looking forward to finding myself again and becoming an even better mom to my children and wife to my husband because I'm a better me."

–LEIGH SABROE, FOUNDER OF THE KID CHRONICLES FACEBOOK PAGE

Table of Contents

Introduction

Is motherhood sucking the joy out of you? Are you overworked, under-appreciated and at times overwhelmed? Do you feel beaten down by the same old routine? If you answered "yes" to any or all of these questions, then this book is for you! Rest assured that if you have a low joy level and really just want to hide from your children, you can create a more meaningful motherhood experience by taking the steps I offer in this book. This guidance is from me, based not only on what I have learned from motherhood, but also on the experiences of countless other mothers on their journey to find their own joy, beyond just caring for their children. It's a journey that takes twists and turns, and even makes u-turns at unexpected times.

Despite all the talk with friends and family and the magazine articles you read, you are never fully prepared for the experience of motherhood. How can you be? It is an experience unlike any other. One that is filled with pure joy, deep love and being pushed beyond your limits of patience and tolerance. It's mixed with your expectations, your childhood experiences, your dreams and your feelings about yourself.

Take a look at yourself right now. Are you strong? Are you satisfied with your life? Are you in a rut? How do you feel about your lover/spouse? Do you have supportive people around you? Are you rigid or open to change? All of these issues play into what your experience as a mother will bring you.

As you read this book, you may find that you're already taking the steps described in some chapters, but you may fall way below the line in taking the steps recommended in other chapters. Please don't worry about that. My goal in writing this book is to have you love your life and be full of joy, not to make you feel unhappy that you lost track of yourself years ago. I wrote this book because I want all mothers to be deeply in love with their lives, both when their children are around and when they are alone. Do you like the company you keep when you are alone? Do you lock yourself in the bathroom to talk on the phone? Oh wait, that's different, I hope you do that. For some of us, that phone call when the kids are on the other side of the locked bathroom door might be the only adult time we get in a 12-hour period.

Motherhood encompasses the toddler years, where all we do is give and chase little legs around, and the physical and emotional exhaustion of handling teenagers with jobs and dating partners. No matter where you are on this beautiful, at times exhausting journey through motherhood, I want you to be happy and have a solid sense of who you are and what gives you joy. Not just the fleeting joy of a warm cup of coffee or a new purse—I mean the deep, heart-nourishing, soul-satisfying joy that comes from within. That is the joy I mean and this book offers you a plan for how to get it. What seems like a lot of work or constant effort is well worth your time in the immediate sense and in the long run. Why does your happiness need to wait until the kids are older and out of the home? Don't put your happiness on hold; be happy right now. Let this book ignite the fire within you and bring you to a place of self-contentment. Your bright light shining will encourage others to want to live the best life they can, too.

CHAPTER 1

How Full Is Your Joy Cup?

"Find the courage to be the best and most joyful woman you can be."
–JULIE McGRATH

....

The most freeing statement—one that set me on the journey back to joy that I hope this book will show you how to make—came to me after I spent the afternoon sobbing tears of frustration in my room. The morning had been a nonstop nagging monologue. "No, Jared, don't eat that. No, Jared, don't touch that. No no no no no…" all day long.

When my toddler finally went down for his nap, I raced to my room, closed the door and had a good long cry to release the day's frustrations. Then I was interrupted by a knock on my front door. I came downstairs, red-eyed and horrified that I was the worst parent in the world for feeling what I was feeling. I didn't like my child at that moment and in fact hadn't even enjoyed his company for weeks. This was an exhausting phase, with a toddler age two years and two months who was touching everything in sight, not listening, forcing me to endlessly chase him to avoid catastrophe. The minute he was up in the morning, so were my husband and I. There were no slow wake-up mornings. I hit the ground running and stayed that way until nighttime, making for long, tiring days.

My friend looked at me, understood right away and uttered that glorious, freeing statement: "You know, Julie, you don't have to like your kids all the time."

What? Really? You mean I can say I don't want to be a mom right now? I don't have to like my kids today?

That was freeing to me. Completely liberating.

You see, I was surrounded by women who gave up their lives for their children. I thought that was what I was supposed to do, too. I knew women who ditched their relationship with their husbands and slept in the same bed as their kids, gave up their hobbies and focused entirely on what made the kid happy. They gave up their favorite jobs and said they were sacrificing their own happiness for their kids' happiness. They forgot what life had been like before kids, and didn't do much that didn't revolve around their kids. Was I destined for the same outcome? To become a shell of what I once was, all because I had a baby?

Before I had children, I had thought every waking moment with them would be glorious. Okay, so I was a bit naïve, but I wasn't around kids much. What did I know? Then when I was bombarded with this range of emotions once I did have my own children, I wasn't sure if I was the problem. How could a mother feel so annoyed at her toddler that she actually started thinking about all the great points of life pre-kids? I was that mother and I knew that in order for me to survive this most precious of journeys in motherhood, I had best surround myself with women who felt this way, too. Surrounding myself with women who gave it all up for their kids would not provide me with the reinforcement I would need as a mother.

I wasn't one of those women who wanted to lose herself completely to her family. In fact, I was the exact opposite. I was sure being a strong, confident woman with a life beyond them would better suit my children than showing them a depleted, tired woman who yelled and became easily frustrated, who no longer nurtured her adult relationship with her husband or went out to enrich her life.

I realized then that knew I required my adult world… coffee dates with friends, hot sex with my husband, time on my own, and work outside the home. I craved this world, needed it for my existence, deserved it, and by God, I was going to reclaim it.

This book will show you how to reclaim yourself as a strong, confident and joyful woman and spell out the steps you need to take to get there. Whether you are a new mom still changing diapers or have teenagers whose activity and work schedules dominate your afternoons, you can have your life, too. You can! And it's never too late.

On airplanes, flight attendants tell you to put the oxygen mask on yourself before you put it on your children. Why? Well, if you can't breathe, how are you going to help your children? That's really what this book is all about. If you are not happy and nourished, how can you reflect those feelings to your children? If you are content and fulfilled in your life (i.e., taking care of yourself, enjoying hobbies and friends), then you are truly and genuinely able to be present, patient and more loving toward your children. If you decide to hand over the oxygen mask to your children and wait for years to put your own on, you will most likely be full of frustration, feeling empty and bored!

This book will show you how to create your life exactly as you want it to be and how to set your goals and dreams in motion while believing it is possible and that you are worthy of every minute of joy coming your way!

There are ladies I have met along the way who have a take-charge personality. When they set their mind to something, they get it. They overcome obstacles, annoyances and even grievances, and give it their all. They make their dreams a reality. We sit back in awe and say, "You were able to do *what*?" Very impressive, you think. Could I possibly do that too?

So you play with that thought in your head for a while, thinking about the tremendous amount of work that would need to take place. The risk involved. The putting yourself out there to go for something that means a lot to you. So you sit back and decide, oh, maybe another time. Now is not the right time. Maybe someday, maybe tomorrow... and days go by, months turn into years and there's still no movement. Life is going by and you are still where you were years ago. No movement. You find yourself watching all those around you get what they want and yet you still sit back, not fully participating in your own life, wondering when it will be your time.

Here is your wake-up call. Life doesn't stop for you and wait until you are feeling ready. Now is your time! If you are waiting for someone to light a fire under your butt to get the ball rolling in the right direction—here it is.

Allow me to light it for you.

Get moving in the direction of your dreams. Your choices reflect how you feel. How much joy can you have when you are stuck, not moving forward, not growing? Ask yourself, are you in love with your life? If not, what do you need to do to get there? What do you need to create in your life that will get you excited to wake up every morning and shout "yes" instead of pulling yourself out of bed, weary and sad, saying it's just another crummy day and tomorrow will be the same and so will the next day. **Stop that vicious cycle of blah.** Only you have the power and the drive to kick-start your life in another, more satisfying direction.

Disclaimer: What you need to know as you read this book is that I truly, deeply love my children. They are my most precious gifts and my supreme joy. I am deeply thankful for each day I have with them. My children are two years apart; deciding to have my second child before life got too easy with my first was a perfectly calculated choice. I knew it would be a hard few years with two young kids, but I knew better than to wait to have a second child until I was on easy street with the first one (sleeping through the night, no diapers). I knew myself, and that I would be reluctant to go back to all the work of an infant.

My boy is a gentle, caring soul and a bright light in my world; he loves trains, plays hockey and goes snowmobiling with his father. My girl is a vivacious, stubborn firecracker who makes me laugh every day with her funny antics. They both exhaust me and thrill me. Our family laughs, screams, cries, decorates the kitchen floor with finger paints, and snorkels in tubs filled with bubble bath. We take hikes in the woods, have car seats filled with crumbled goldfish crackers and a deep faith in God. We are blessed with a constant flow of family and friends who make our lives sparkle. Our house is the go-to house in the summertime; we buy a huge inflatable water slide, pack the coolers and spend the afternoons with all of our friends in the sun, happy afternoons giving way to bonfire nights of roasting marshmallows and messy s'mores. These are the times I feel most nourished, watching the children play and be loved not just by me, but by the support group I have built.

But it wasn't always this way. At one point, when my son was two and my daughter was just a cranky, colicky baby, I felt isolated, angry and frustrated. Despite being told, "Having children is so rewarding," it was anything but. Most days I'd yell out to no one in particular, "Still waiting for the rewards here!" Mornings were spent planning how to survive the many hours until bedtime. How many hours can I kill if I give her two baths and three walks around the block?

I felt like I had no purpose. Changing diapers and feeding the kids every few hours was making me feel like a zombie. My husband did his best. When my daughter decided to change her sleep pattern at age one, he would quietly take her every night and sleep on the couch so I wouldn't lose my mind. It was the worst three months of my life, not one full night of sleep. Since I'm someone who needs eight if not nine solid hours of shut-eye to think clearly, I was a mess. But it passed, just like my friends told me it would. They encouraged me to hang in there, it will all pass, and it did.

I found friends who supported me with kind words and invited me to their homes to offer love and praise. And I ate it all up and it brightened my days, kept me going. And then soon after, my children were in daycare, and then transitioned to school. A solid six hours of child care that I didn't have to manage. And although I feel now like I am on easy street, there are still moments when I scream, yell and try to hold it together. That's the real part of motherhood. There are the beautiful, exciting times when your kid wins a trophy or smothers you with kisses. There are the real, hard-core parenting times when you want to have a down-and-dirty brawl on the kitchen floor with your husband about who gets to do an errand first and escape the madness, called "children running wild," in your home. This book is honest about the ups and downs of parenting and offers you tools for better preparing yourself to put some of that passion for your own life back into your being. You will often hear me say how you truly deserve to be happy and are worthy of all good things in life. But you must plan accordingly. If you are not a planner, start now. Get organized, grab a calendar and start marking the days for *your* joy.

For example, when my husband leaves for a long weekend trip with his snowmobiling friends, instead of being alone with my children for three to four days with no breaks, I budget ahead of time for babysitters each day. This gets me three to four hours of coffee with friends, a walk in the woods or just an extra set of hands. Do you see what I mean about planning? Think ahead. Strategize about how you will get (and pay for if necessary) your own fun and excitement without children. This book offers a new view of parenting, one that argues for having a great, satisfying life while you parent your children.

Here's an example. Once, when we were having construction work done on our home, I was lying out in the yard with my iPod and a glass of iced tea. The carpenter said to me, "Let me get this straight, you have a babysitter inside with the kids while you are lying outside in the sun?" "Hell, yes," I laughed. "My children will thank me for it later when I have more patience in dealing with them."

If I am only afforded two hours to myself all weekend, what should I be doing with my precious two hours? Laundry? Cleaning? Would that nourish me and renew me for spending the rest of the weekend of chasing my three- and five-year-olds? Come on, ladies, be smarter than your children and give yourself a break. Don't you deserve one? Let me re-phrase that statement: *you deserve one!* While I don't know you personally, I do know that mothers need breaks from their mothering duties to relax and be in the company of someone other than their children. Laugh. Dream. Take up line dancing. Kayak down the river (just remember to come back up the river, since some days it's tempting to keep on going).

This book is based on my own experiences once I married and became a mother, and on the experiences of the women I have worked with as a coach and social worker. The expectations society has for women once they take on these very important roles are very different than they are for men who are "married with children." As women, we must fight for our time to be whole, to be complete and to be nourished, because all of that does *not* come from being with our children. In this book, I share the wisdom gleaned from my conversations with the hundreds of women I have worked with and been friends with about their experiences raising children, having tough in-laws, wrestling with life-work balance issues and losing themselves in the process.

Throughout the book, there are reflective questions called "Journal Entries" to assist you in your quest for reclaiming your joy. You can write the answers in this book, or in a notebook or journal that becomes your own "Joy Journal." You can also go to my website and download these questions if you would prefer not to write in the book or a journal. They can be found on my website: www.thejoysource.com/joy-worthy-guide/ (username: HappyMom, password: BESTLIFE).

A little about my life journey so far, so you know where I'm coming from.
In my twenties, I was always looking for an exciting adventure, traveling and meeting new people, and I thought I was pretty confident and prepared for the adventure of "married with children." I had travelled to Central America, immersed myself in a new culture and excelled. My professional life as a social worker had me stabilizing the most troubled families in the most challenging inner-city housing projects in Florida. If I could teach those mothers how to love, nurture and maintain their families, surely my own adjustment to parenting would be a breeze. Right?

Wrong!

When I became a mother, I was surprised by how much I learned about myself as a woman and how much I had to learn. The experience of becoming a mother changed me in very profound ways and led me to my journey of self-discovery.

I eventually learned I had two choices: take good care of myself or perish.

When I finally realized I could choose to stay focused on myself or risk being lost forever, I chose the first option.

It took a lot of work, but I chose *me*.

You see, the patience you need with small children, the endless nights of not sleeping and the tantrums of even the most well-adjusted children can all push anyone to the brink of losing it. Anyone! And we all find ourselves at the brink. We all lose ourselves (and our minds) at one time or another, especially during the early years of motherhood. You have a tiny, living person completely dependent on you, so it's natural to devote all your time, energy, thoughts and behaviors to that amazing creation.

But how do you hold it all together and not lose yourself completely in the process? Is that even possible? I am telling you it *is* possible. It takes work and an open mind. It takes a sense of humor only a mom understands and it takes being real with yourself and about your situation. I am known for telling it like it is; I won't sugarcoat my difficult days. There are times when being a parent is hard and you just need a break from the whining, the questions, the Wiggles. Some of us feel guilty even *saying* that, never mind doing it.

I not only say it, but I do it. When I feel the daily grind of homework, laundry, errands and chores bogging me down, I book myself a weekend away. My dear friend Kelly and I make sure we do at least two "girlfriend weekends" per year. Sometimes it is just for one night, but for that one night, I am just me, Julie the person, not Julie the mother, the wife, the go-to person. Every so often I leave by myself for a week to rejuvenate my spirit so I can reenter the busy world of motherhood refreshed. I remember when I first traveled to California alone; the airplane ride was a glorious five hours where no one spoke to me and asked anything of me. I was free to just think and move at my own pace. If you are shocked to read this, thinking "that's great for her but I could never do that," please keep reading, my friend.

Maybe you can start small, just by taking a few hours to yourself. We are all different in how we parent and what our comfort level is about leaving our family for a night or two. If it doesn't feel right for you to leave your family for an overnight, then don't. I am certainly not encouraging you to make choices that make you feel worse. Self-care, as we will discuss in detail in this book, is about doing what makes you feel good. Maybe just a night out with friends or a quiet jog through the woods will refresh you enough. But we all need to practice self-care to be strong, confident women, and to keep growing and getting better.

Staying stagnant and marinating in the juices of tiredness and depletion is no longer an option for you! The solution goes well beyond taking a hot bath or getting a massage to feel better; I will explain to you the entire process for feeling whole and complete. Beyond my own life and professional experience, I have spent months doing research on resilience, optimism and self-fulfillment. In this book, I share with you all that I have learned and am now implementing in my own life. I want you to be so deeply in love with your own life that you can't imagine living anyone else's. This path involves growth, expansion and risks, so be prepared. The journey back to joy is not always easy or comfortable, but the rewards of feeling completely nourished and self-confident will be well worth it.

This book can help you no matter what stage of parenting you are in, so jump in and enjoy the journey! Read it during your quiet time, carve out those much-needed moments of "you" time and reflect on your own journey in motherhood. Again, I've provided journal entry questions throughout the book for you to complete and reflect upon. I suggest finding a nice journal to accompany your adventure through this book. My hope is that reading this book and reflecting on these questions will open up thoughts and dreams that you never knew you had (or have not acknowl-edged). I hope you will be inspired to find the courage to be the best and most joyful woman you can be.

You will notice that integrated in every chapter is the topic of surrounding yourself with healthy, positive friends. Such friends are essential for living a full, exciting life. Seek them out if you don't already have them. I hope this book will help you challenge your fears and lead to growth and forward movement in such a way that your ordinary days will be transformed into extraordinary ones. Give yourself permission to seek growth and passion in your life without being held back by fear and guilt over what society says a "good mother should do."

Because who ever said a "good mother" should cease being a strong, confident woman?

Before you move on to the next chapter, let's start with your own personal Joy Rating. Is your personal joy cup half-full or half-empty?

When it comes to joy, do you feel you:

>> Have it?

>> Are almost there?

>> Are far from it?

>> Need some serious help in finding joy?

We are all in different places when it comes to how much or how little joy we have in our lives right now. This book offers you guidance on getting to a place of joy, living in this world with your joy cup full and overflowing.

CHAPTER 2

Children Enter the Mix:
You Feel Blessed... and Tired

"Did I ever believe I would be up all night tending to a sick kid, cradling her in my arms like an angel, looking down at her amazed at what a perfect creature she was... and spend another day lying in bed, too exhausted to move, thinking 'Is this really what I signed up for?' I can't stand anyone in my family today, and I really want to make up a late work meeting so I don't have to come home and face the nightly routine of bath and bed one more time."

–JULIE McGRATH

If you're reading this book, you have welcomed a child into your life, whether by adoption, birth or foster care. Maybe you "worked" for this "gift"… nights of wonderful, sexy lovemaking, or days of endless fertility treatments or meetings with social workers. Or maybe it was one drunk night and a surprise "oops." No matter how this child was created and what you did to bring him or her into your life…

You, my friend, are now a mother.

For some women, motherhood has been a lifelong dream. For others, it's been a passing thought or a horrid fear. I know women who were born to breed, and others who probably should've had their tubes tied at age thirteen.

We spend our years watching mothers, from women in our own circle to national figures to characters on television sitcoms. We wonder, "Would I be more patient and kind like Carol Brady from the 'Brady Bunch' or like the mom from 'Malcolm in the Middle'? How would I parent? Like my parents parented me?" We watch others with kids and think, "I would do that differently, that kid would not be acting up if she were *my* kid." Of course, this is too funny, because it all changes once you have kids.

It is so easy to judge others when you don't have kids. I once went to a friend's home. Her son was cradled on her lap, sleeping, she was relaxing, and I thought, "Oh, the joys of motherhood, I want that too, all her days must be like that." Boy, I was in for a surprise! Now I am trying to remember if I ever had more than a few idyllic moments like that. Moments, that is, not days. The minute the baby comes out, it is an instant love affair. You see this beautiful baby and your life will never be the same—and it will be full of mixed emotions.

Infants: Sweet Bundles of Joy or Tiny Hungry Leeches?

As I carried my infant in public, I would often hear, "Don't you just wish they stayed young like that?" I would think to myself "Oh, my God, no!" That was not my wish!

The infant stage was not my favorite at all. I was so happy to see both my children grow into little people who could talk, tell me when they felt upset or when their tummy hurt, and play and dream.

I remember attempting to breast-feed my son, but one month was all I could handle. My son was always hungry; I would feed him all morning until my breasts were aching and raw. I then would travel two miles to see my mom, my boy would fuss and she would say, "I think he is hungry." And I would burst into tears. "How could he possibly be hungry, he was attached to my breast all morning!" He was on me all day and despite the push for breast-feeding as "the only way to feed your baby," I was all done. There was another, happier, more pleasant way for me: get the kid a bottle. Luckily I got my insurance company to pay for all the formula, so I could spend my money on the huge quantities of diapers I had to buy each week. I do realize that breast-feeding offers a wonderful experience of connection for many women, and I have heard those moments are amazing. But they are not right or attainable for everyone. The larger point here is that no single option is right for every mother and baby.

Every stage of parenting gets better than the last. But did you ever think it would be this much work? Were you warned? I wasn't. In fact, I felt misled. The parenting magazines I read always showed a happy mom with her kids. I thought it was going to be easier than it actually was. Before my son was born, I figured I'd get that baby on a nap schedule right away and have him sleeping through the night so I could return to being the capable, confident woman I was prior to this baby invading my uterus and life. Hah! Shame on me for being so naïve.

Being a mother is a lot of work; depending on the ages of your children, it is physical, emotional or both. When you work hard at parenting and give it your all, you are tired! There are many definitions of what constitutes "good" parenting, find your own. Be open to new ideas and come to terms with the fact that not every option is right for you. Just because your friend swears by diaper wipe warmers doesn't mean you have to buy one. Parent the way your personality draws you to. There are so many variations and styles. Parent well and love those children with your heart and soul. A colleague warned me, "You can't undo bad parenting," and I believed him. I didn't want to be a bad parent. Motherhood is the oldest profession in the history of the world (other than prostitution, which, ironically, requires some similar activities). I believed I had one shot to get parenting right and I thought I could succeed with no problem; I just had to give it all of me. So when I was totally exhausted at the end of the day, I believed I was doing right by my child.

WRONG!

Remember that song "Running on Empty" by Jackson Browne? That's how I consistently felt when my children were young.

There's never enough internal juice when you are up at night doing feedings, tending to nightmares, waking up early with no slow starts and jumping right in to being "on" as a parent. If you work outside the home, you try to switch into your professional persona while getting the little one ready and just as you are getting into the car either you discover you forgot their lunch or the baby has filled up another diaper, causing more delays. Rarely do you get to work on time and in a good mindset (and without some sort of stain on your shirt).

**"Don't worry kids, mommy doesn't have a favorite.
You all annoy me equally."**

—LEIGH SABROE, THE KID CHRONICLES FACEBOOK PAGE

Coming home is no picnic either. The "witching hours" between four and six p.m., when kids are cranky and hungry, used to drive me to tears. Do you give in and just feed them snacks so you can have peace? Or do you secretly go upstairs and cry in the shower just to let it all out?

Let me differentiate between good exhaustion and bad exhaustion. The good exhaustion comes from being an active parent: riding bikes, planting a garden together, training for a marathon together. The bad exhaustion comes from only doing for them: being a "mom taxi" with a one-way pass to depletion on every level. Bad exhaustion stems from overloading your kids with too many sports or activities and trying to keep up with it all. Try to get away from bad exhaustion and aim for good exhaustion. Being an active parent is much different from giving all to your children and doing nothing for yourself. Active and involved parents are tired at day's end because they enjoyed playing with their kids, not because they have been sucked dry by their children's needs.

As children get older, the challenges are just as demanding and exhausting. Do I even get one minute to myself? (You do when you hire great babysitters, but we'll get into that in another chapter.) My husband and I would joke, "How could one tiny child exhaust two grown adults so much?"

Let's face it, ladies, for most of us, here is where the tide turns in the wonderful marriage we agreed to, for better or worse. We get most of the "worse" part. We become the caregiver, the maid, the wife, the mother, the confidante, the secretary, the taxi driver and many other exciting roles! Who knew? And somehow even the best husbands don't quite share the load enough.

If you are a high-energy, well-organized person like me, you do five tasks to your spouse's one. I'm not sure how we keep it all in our heads, but we know and track schedules, birthdays, bills to be paid, clothes that are outgrown, dinner menus and school stuff. All in our heads, all at once.

Our spouses work, they come home, maybe coach a sports game or two, and think they are pulling as much of the family load as we are. I appreciate good, dedicated fathers because I had one. I encourage my spouse to do as much as I do, as much as possible. For some, it can come with a fight, but it's one that's worth the effort.

> If you fight for equality as soon as the baby comes out, the road ahead will be easier on you. Remember, you're a team, and communication is how this team works.

Women often run circles around their men, but we also know we can handle all the details. It comes naturally and we are good at it. Do I shovel snow and do the yard work? No. That's why my husband and I are a good match. We each have our designated chores that only one of us does, as well as chores that we share.

I am not husband-bashing, believe me. I have a fantastic husband who helps as much as I instruct him to. But after 10 years he can't quite remember that on Wednesdays, if we don't do the kids' laundry, there will be no clean socks or underwear on Friday. Sometimes I want to rebel; I see the laundry and don't do it. I have other important things to do, dammit, and it's his turn this week. But more times than most, if I don't do it, it doesn't get done.

So yes, once you have children, your relationship with your spouse will become very lopsided, if it isn't already. You are the one on the bottom holding up the world. Remembering every last detail about every child, and your home, and your child's friends and their homes... and on and on.

> Tip: Hire a housecleaner; your "free" time is best spent on self-care. Don't spend a Saturday dusting and cleaning the toilets. Housecleaning services are cheap and if you budget for it, even if it is monthly, it is well worth it. On the weekends, prepare big dinner casseroles that you throw in the oven on the weekdays.

Parenting is tough work—the discipline, the homework, the diapers. Did you ever think you and your husband would keep a mental note of who gets what time off? We found ourselves comparing… Well, you got six hours of sleep last night, I only got four, or you went out last night so I get that hour to myself. Yes, we kept score. And when my daughter was a finicky baby we fought to get out of the house to do the food shopping. Ahhh, you know it's bad when Sunday morning alone at the grocery store seems like paradise.

The Toddler Years: Non-Stop Sound and Motion

 You longed for them to start walking and talking, now sometimes you just wish they would sit down and shut up. When my kids were very young and up early on the weekends, we would go to our neighbor's house so our kids could play with their young kids. We'd all be sitting outside at seven-thirty on a Saturday morning, eyes half-open, drinking coffee and sharing a few laughs to ease the pain. We secretly glared with envy at other neighbors who had already been through the early years of child-rearing and who could now come and go with ease, even have the luxury of sleeping past six. I confess I often hated them.

In my world, having two toddlers meant being up all night cleaning vomit from the carpet or tending to a child's fever that kept me awake every hour with anxiety. Or better yet, changing wet beds twice in one night. The days were spent answering the same questions over and over again, or hearing "Mommy mommy mommy mommy

I want I want I want." Potty training and preschool. Making safe every place we visited that was not already child-proofed.

"Embarrassing Mommy Moment #698,764: You know you're a full-fledged mommy when after a full day of running errands you finally return home, pass a mirror and gasp as you realize you have not one, but four crushed Cocoa Krispies cemented to the ass of your pants... and you weren't even the one who ate cereal for breakfast today. Humiliation at its finest, but at least now all those random disgusted stares I received in my travels today make a bit more sense..."

–WHERE'S THE FU*#KING MOMMY MANUAL?

During the toddler years, my self-care routine meant splurging for nice, hot coffee at our local coffee shop. That was what got me through many weekends. Yup, hot, beautiful, savory coffee and neighbors who felt the same way about parenting (and coffee). I loved those moments when my son took my face in both his jelly-smeared hands and said, "Mommy, I love you."

Yet, I longed for my Monday mornings like nobody's business. Weekends were all work and Mondays it was back to *me*; I couldn't wait to get to work with adults and use my professional talents. After a long weekend with plenty of family time, the thought of being home on a Monday doing the childcare routine all over again would send me over the edge. I enjoyed dressing up and being with adults all day. I went to graduate school for a reason: to work in a professional setting and use my gifts. I love my kids but I also know myself; come Monday morning, I need to be someplace other than where they are. I know many amazing, patient, creative mothers who spend free time doing crafts with their young children or who can think up a cool variety show routine for their teenager. All good. We have different talents. My point is, don't compare yourself to other women around you and feel you are somehow lacking because you don't do crafts or you don't work outside the home. We all have and use different talents; discover what brings you joy.

The Elementary School Years: Another Shift

 This is the stage when your children start to realize you aren't their entire world (and for some of us, when math once again makes you feel like an idiot).

Finally, you have reached the stage of dropping all the kids off at the same school and not seeing them again until late afternoon. Wow, is that a mixed blessing. They are in "big kid" school, no longer with you all day nor in the comfortable, safe daycare that you have used since they were infants. Mixed feelings indeed. I made it a habit to attend all the classroom parties so I could get to know all the kids and meet the parents. Be involved. It makes all the difference.

> "No Monday school morning is complete without you yelling at your kid and causing them to crumble into a ball of tears because school starts in five minutes and there is simply no more time left to continue the rescue and recovery search for a bunny stuffed animal she hasn't seen in over four months but desperately needs right now."
>
> –WHERE'S THE FU*#KING MOMMY MANUAL?

The magic years of ages five through ten are when my children still believed in Santa, the tooth fairy and the Easter bunny. For me, the expression on their faces when they came down the stairs on Christmas morning made having kids all worth it. The energy they gave off, of excitement and innocence, is what I fed on. Beautiful, pure blissful energy that so many of us adults no longer have within us. It was all magic and I enjoyed every minute and I hope you do (or did), too.

Do you know the feeling when you see your children engage in an activity they love so much? They glow from the inside. It is our job as parents not to buy them stuff but to engage in fun experiences with them. We need to notice what they are naturally good at and then encourage them to participate in it. Not push, insult, or demean, but encourage, love and get excited. We are all born with natural abilities and interests;

find out what your kid loves to do and get them there. Your child will be so full of positive energy and a sense of fulfillment. These are the kids who are the happiest and most whole. Not the kids who get everything bought for them and have no inner substance at all. Those are the spoiled brats who constantly need stuff to make them feel whole. **Don't set your kid up for a lifetime of buying, shopping and objects; there won't be enough "stuff" in this universe to make them feel complete inside.**

Start now. Experiences, hobbies, interests, volunteering, all these make a person feel complete and enough. In my Joy Course, I talk in detail about being hardy as an adult and how hardy individuals are resilient. Our goal as parents is to build resilient children. Why? Children who are dedicated to their own wellbeing, to others, to their family, and to their faith will work hard and have better life satisfaction. They don't fall apart when life throws them a curveball. If you don't feel you match this description of resilience, I am happy you are reading this book. Don't pass the unhappiness on to your children. There are some qualities you can't help (premature graying, poor tooth structure, unibrow), but you can instill happiness, optimism, and gratitude in your children. Find these qualities in yourself first. Once you have them, they spill over to your children.

The extracurricular activity debate is something you'll hear over and over again in every circle of mothers. Sometimes it's more of a complaint session than a debate: "I am a taxi! All I do is bring him to all his activities every day, I am exhausted!" How much is too much? One or two activities per child running concurrently is more than enough. Why over schedule? Why sign him up for three or four activities/sports at one time? It's nonsense and not necessary. It creates a hectic, chaotic schedule that is not pleasurable to anyone. Parents feel the pressure to sign their children up for everything. Resist that—it's so much better for everyone in the family to choose a few activities/sports you know your child will love and keep it at that.

One year my son had Boy Scouts and it was either choose hockey or Sunday school for his second activity. I joke that I chose hockey over God. I can give God at home every day, but I couldn't give him hockey at home. What would be the point of rushing him from place to place on a Sunday morning when I rush him out to school every weekday morning? Kids need downtime just like we adults do. It is important for them to have time to play in their rooms, in the yard and with their friends, to be unscheduled and creative.

The Tween and Teen Years

 Ah, "Tweens"—you love them and hate them all at once, and you might even need a self-help group to get through this stage. Puberty starts, and with it comes the attitude, the bras, the periods, the mood swings, the love for the pop star of the moment. "There is not enough alcohol in the world to see me through this stage," jokes my friend Janna. Her daughter went from sweet girl to witchy woman in the course of a school year. Clothing became very important, along with cell phones, texting, and who likes who—and Janna does her best to keep up with it all. "I read all texts and emails that my daughter sends and receives." Kids can be so cruel using the new social media. It only takes one mistake like sending an inappropriate photo to a boy and the entire city will see it and down goes a girl's reputation.

Teenagers are the big-attitude pimpled people of entitlement who want to use your car and leave it on empty. They want all the new gadgets, phones and a car. They sleep until noon, would rather drink juice from the carton than pour a glass, and throw their clothes on the floor. Dating, the "serious sex talk," birth control and driver safety are just a few of the fun topics you will find yourself discussing in this stage.

It's not all a headache: in fact, some of the best vacations are when teenagers are in the picture. Jillian and her husband take their three teenagers on vacation every year and both she and her husband actually enjoy themselves. Imagine that! When you raise happy, healthy, smart children, they make good choices and allow the adults to be at ease. For some people, like my friend Maria, the true bonding began when her daughter was a teenager.

"Since her father was not in her life, we grew closer every year," said Maria. "As she got older and more mature, our relationship blossomed. This was the best stage yet! Being a single mother was so tiring when she was younger. Honestly, I wanted her to grow up. I know my friends wish they were still tucking their children into bed, but those were not great years for me. I worked full-time and was worn to the bone. My friends are envious of our relationship, and I watch as they struggle with out-of-control children. I was thankful I allowed her freedom with my trust and she never betrayed it. We both have an adventurous spirit and take time planning local and far-away adventures. She considers me a cool mother and that makes me so happy."

Rules and structure are huge for teenagers and make for a happier mother. Mothers who are hunting down their daughter in the middle of the night at some random boy's home or bailing their kid out of jail have it tough. Stress, anxiety and worry become part of the everyday. Remember, it is very difficult to undo bad parenting. Creating and sticking to rules is a MUST. Kids who have jobs, healthy friends and hobbies are happier kids.

It's usually very easy to get little children excited—just point at a fire truck going by and their faces light up. As they grow older, it is up to us to ensure that our children maintain a growing excitement about their life. They need to be able to find excitement in everyday activities, like doing their best in sports games, hiking, going on mini-vacations, or connecting with friends. The trick is to not get caught up in the trap that happiness has to cost a lot of money.

Most kids will beg for the same expensive toys and gadgets that their friends have. That's where you come in. I don't mind buying my son a bike that is a bit expensive, since he loves biking, it's great exercise and he uses it all summer long. To me that is a good investment. What's not a good investment is $100 sneakers just because they are the brand that happens to be in style this month.

Kids will take direction from you on where you seek joy. If you are busy buying the latest and the greatest but still never appear happy, they most likely will do the same. If you spend all your time in front of the television, eating unhealthy food, your children will learn from you. In a later chapter, I spend more time discussing how and where to get this joy for yourself as an adult. When there's excitement in your home about birthdays, perfect spelling tests and making the soccer team, you are feeding your kids with good, positive emotions. Encouraging your kids to have hobbies they enjoy will provide them with lasting joy.

The book *Flow* discusses teenagers and the concept of total enjoyment in life. The term "flow" is what author Mihaly Csikszentmihalyi uses to describe being one with the activity because you enjoy it so much. You'll have happier teens if they have more opportunities to experience "flow" moments through work and interests that engage them.

Flow moments are moments when time stops, where we are totally one with what we are doing, and these moments produce life satisfaction. The concept is explored in detail by Csikszentmihalyi in *Flow*, which is about joy, creativity, and the process of total involvement in life. The more "flow" moments in our lives, the better off we will be. Here's why, as Martin Seligman explains in his book *Authentic Happiness*:

"In one of [Csikszentmihalyi's] studies he tracked 250 high-flow teenagers and 250 low-flow teenagers. The low-flow teenagers are 'mall' kids; they hang out at malls and they watch television a lot. The high-flow kids have hobbies, they engage in sports, and they spend a lot of time on homework. On every measure of psychological wellbeing (including self-esteem and engagement) save one, the high-flow teenagers did better. The exception is important: the high-flow kids think their low-flow peers are having more fun, and say they would rather be at the mall doing all those 'fun' things or watching television. But while all the engagement they have is not perceived as enjoyable, it pays off later in life. The high-flow kids are the ones who make it to college, who have deeper social ties, and whose later lives are more successful. This fits [his] theory that flow is a state that builds psychological capital that can be drawn on in the years to come."

Children with Special Needs

 Children who require extra attention bring a new set of challenges. Not only do you have the normal day-to-day challenges but also additional worries, doctor's appointments and many medications. Whether it is a physical, emotional or learning disability or all of the above, children with disabilities or special needs can add stress and tension to your life and your marriage. I encourage mothers to check out local resource centers where they can find answers to any of their questions, read up on the latest therapies and medications, and attend workshops. Hospitals are a great place to start. Most have resource centers for parents.

Pretending that your child is fine, when instinctually you know he's not, doesn't help anyone. In fact, it prolongs the helping process and does your child a disservice. Reaching out to your pediatrician or your child's school is the first step. Getting help for yourself is the second, and they both go hand in hand. You need support, too. The extra resources it takes to handle your special-needs child can exhaust *you* physically and emotionally.

Dee is the mother of three boys; her oldest, Nathan, is mentally challenged and blind. Because he is mild-mannered and surrounded by extended family who help and support them in tremendous ways, Dee believes she has it good. She will never complain or wish it were different. When Nathan was a baby, she did need to see a therapist to help her gain the strength necessary to support her child with a lifetime of care. She will tell you her son is a true gift from God; he is all love, innocence and sweetness—but also total care. She does accept breaks when her parents agree to sit for a night or two. She doesn't feel an ounce of guilt, because they love him and know how to care for him. Every three months or so she needs to take the weekend off and recharge her batteries. She doesn't try to be a martyr, because she would just crash and burn if she was giving all the time and never taking a break.

Children offer us love, laughter and amazing hugs. Each stage of their development brings a deeper love for them and new headaches. If you are unable to take a break from your children, you will not be able to appreciate the rewards of motherhood. It becomes too draining a process if you are unable to be fully yourself and fully a mother. It is very possible to do both. Don't miss those amazing moments you can never get back. Don't get caught up with trying to buy them all the toys and gadgets. Spend as little time as possible with women who brag and spoil their children with expensive toys and clothing. I have been in fancy homes that look like museums and have the love energy of a library. Newsflash: Stuff does not equal love.

Dance and sing with your children. Talk with your teenager. Hug your 19-year-old boy. Smooch your spouse. Hold hands and run through the sprinkler all together. Don't strive for the perfect home to impress people. Create your home your way, semi-organized, semi-clean and filled with a lot of love. My children were ages eight and six before they each had a room of their own, and not once did they ask why they didn't each have their own rooms. It wasn't important to them—they shared (most of the time) and expected his stuff to be in her stuff and there were no territorial issues.

As each stage of parenting brings its own set of challenges, frustrations, joys and surprises, a home with an abundance of love and a strong mother will make the transitions from one age to the next easier and more manageable. All the more reason to read on to learn how to be a strong, confident mother who loves your children without giving up love for yourself. **There is plenty of love to go around; please don't stop it at your children and your spouse; keep it flowing back to yourself.** When you take a break from the daily routine of homework, chores and the chaos of shuttling kids to sporting events, you can see your kids in a whole new light. When you take your kids for a hike in the woods, sit in their room and play card games or go on a family vacation, you gain a new perspective. Stepping away from the hustle and bustle and really seeing your children as bright lights, you get that full feeling of love and contentment. When we take a break from the feeling that family life is sometimes a "burden" and at times, full of stress, we truly appreciate our children. As you will read in the next chapter, stress adds to the pressure of raising healthy, well-adjusted children and at times can take a toll on your health and your happiness.

CHAPTER 3

Warning Lights Are Flashing: Are You Stressed?

Major Aging Accelerators
1. Obesity • 2. Smoking • 3. Stress
–20 YEARS YOUNGER BY BOB GREENE, 2011

I'm tired, stressed and annoyed, The End. Does this sound like something you've said recently?

Some level of stress is an inevitable part of life. We all get stressed for different reasons, based on our perceptions. In order to be stressed in a negative way, you have to view your situation, problem or experience to be beyond your ability to cope with it. What stresses me out might not stress you out. You may love cooking a five-course meal for your in-laws, but the thought of doing that would stress the hell out of me.

I am not going to claim you will never have stress. With life comes stress. What I explain in this chapter is what unhealthy stress looks and feels like so you can be aware of the signs and symptoms and do something about it. Why do you need to do something about unhealthy stress? Because it's dangerous and it just plain feels bad—and it gets in the way of your joy. Trust me, if you have someone dependent on you, baby, you have stress coming out your ears. Children add stress to your life. Homework, making lunches, boyfriends/girlfriends, activities, college, finding money for activities and college. The list goes on and on.

journal entry

Warning Lights: When Do You Need a Break?

Do you know the signs within yourself that your stress level is too high?

_____

_____

_____

_____

Do you feel in your body when you need a break from your normal busy routine?

_____

_____

_____

Do you know that stress actually keeps excess weight on your body?

_____

_____

If you are trying hard to lose weight, being stressed will not help you reach your goal. That's because when you are stressed, your body won't metabolize food correctly and you won't lose the weight off those hips (or anywhere else, for that matter!).

According to Dr. Sherrie Bourg Carter, author of the book *High Octane Women*:

"Our bodies provide the first clues to us that our stress levels are too high. When stress throws us off balance physically, our bodies react with signals to let us know that something is wrong." She also notes: "Some signals are **missed** and **minimized**. Some you see and decide not to attend to. But they are always there, usually flashing brightly, but often ignored."

Do any of these symptoms of stress sound familiar to you? Physiological symptoms of stress include:

>> Headaches

>> Indigestion

>> Muscle aches

>> Pounding of the heart

>> Shortness of breath

>> Digestive changes, such as constipation or diarrhea

Do you have any of the above symptoms that you are blaming on reading without your glasses or drinking too much coffee?

Psychological symptoms of stress include:

>> Feelings of helplessness, hopelessness or worthlessness

>> Feelings of being misunderstood or unappreciated

>> Anxiety

>> Anger

>> Defensiveness

>> Depression

>> Difficulty concentrating

- ≫ Hypersensitivity
- ≫ Insecurity
- ≫ Irritability
- ≫ Lack of direction
- ≫ Apathy

Behavioral symptoms of stress include:
- ≫ Increased smoking
- ≫ Increased use of alcohol or drugs
- ≫ Nail biting
- ≫ Changes in eating habits
- ≫ Increased acne
- ≫ Neglect of responsibility
- ≫ Decreased sexual activity
- ≫ Poor job performance
- ≫ Unusually poor hygiene

And the list goes on. I often observe irritability and defensiveness in people when they are stressed. This makes for a not-so-fun person. Think of those "road rage" people who want to stab someone because they were cut off in traffic. Were their stress levels at an all-time high and did they just snap?

Don't let your stress reach such dangerous levels. Not only does it make you unhappy, it also wreaks havoc on your internal organs. Stress involves mind, body, and spirit; not dealing with it can cause catastrophic physical results, like high blood pressure, stroke and heart attack. Learn from the story of my good friend Katie, who is a strong and secure woman. She works full-time, coaches her son's basketball team and manages her husband's business for a few hours each night. She thought she was taking care of herself; spending time reading and taking nights out with friends. Then one night she had such severe chest pains she asked her husband to take her to the emergency room. She had no idea what was happening, since she thought she was in good health, is not overweight and eats well. She spent hours in the emergency room, getting tests and feeling very scared.

Turns out, she was not having a heart attack, but she was stressed. Later, we sat together to figure out what warning signs she had missed and how her lifestyle needed to change. She decided there were things she needed to put back in her life, including jogging, massage and minimizing the chores that only she did around the house (she hired a housecleaner, too). Allowing her husband to take a more active role in her son's after-school activities gave her more time and meant she was doing less "running on empty."

journal entry

Stress

How does stress affect you?

_____

_____

_____

_____

_____

_____

_____

Do you feel it physically? Emotionally? Both?

_____

_____

_____

_____

Stress (continued)

Do you grab an extra coffee, smoke a cigarette and eat greasy fast foods?

_____

_____

_____

Can you link it to your stressful moments?

_____

_____

_____

> "People fight fatigue with coffee, tea, caffeinated drinks, cigarettes, alcohol, and high-fat food. Stimulants further weaken the body and create greater imbalance."
>
> —*THE INNER GAME OF STRESS*, W. TIMOTHY GALLWEY

I see it all the time at the coffee shop. "I will have the extra-tall grande latte with three shots of espresso, five sugars and extra cream." That will keep you up for a while! When you run at a fast pace, not sleeping, not eating healthy, full of stress and anxiety, you crash and burn *hard*. Some of us think we can keep up the accelerated pace indefinitely. This delusion keeps us sharp and everyone looks at us thinking we are supermoms. It will catch up with you, I promise. It is best to take care of yourself now, recognize the signs of symptoms of stress and mitigate them.

Stress Reducers

 According to experts, the number one stress reducer is… (drum roll please) EXERCISE! For those of us who have a daily exercise routine, we not only believe it, we live it. After a hard workout, we feel great. When you have a difficult day, take a walk, or get on that elliptical and let it all out. Push all that anger, frustration and stress right out of you. Notice how you feel afterwards. Calm. Less stressed.

Surrounding yourself with good friends who really know you can prevent a stress disaster waiting to happen. True friends care for us and genuinely look out for our best interests. They will notice when you are at a maximum stress level and they will tell you that you are about to lose your mind and advise you to slow down before you burn out of your life. If you hang around with superficial people, they won't tell you that, because when you are down and out, they rise up and take your place. They are waiting for you to come face-to-face with an all-time stress high. Be with those who love you and don't get defensive if your husband tells you that you seem bitchy, moody, quick to fight, quick to snap. It is his way of telling you, *slow it down.*

When my friend hurt her knee and had to take time off from exercise, she boldly told me, "The exercise is not so much for this (pointing to her butt and thighs) as it is for this" (pointing to her head). Exercise is not only physical, it's mental, and it makes you mental if you love to work out and have to stop for some reason.

So get moving, my lady friend, get that butt in gear and start sweating. Any type of exercise will do. In fact, according to an article by John Bartholomew in *USA Weekend* about research on exercise and stress, "every form of physical activity has been demonstrated to produce a reduction in feelings of anxiety and negative moods." He adds, "the data suggests that people who exercise in the morning, for example, will have less of an increase in blood pressure and less of a feeling of stress if they are in a traffic jam on their way to work."

What are your stress reducers? Do you have a healthy plan for those high-stress days? In addition to exercise, try some of these:

>> Hang out with good friends and laugh

>> Go for a massage

>> Take a hot bath

>> Pat your dog or cat

>> Play with your children (or someone else's children)

>> Read a book

>> Write in your journal

>> Sing as loud as you can

>> Engage in your hobby

>> Watch a funny movie

Laughter is often the best medicine. Research has shown that laughing lowers stress hormones (like cortisol, epinephrine and adrenaline) and strengthens the immune system by releasing health-enhancing hormones.

There are clear links between stress, happiness and health. "Research shows that stressors at work weaken the immune system on the day they occur. Pleasant events enhanced the immune system for up to two days," according to *The Psychology of Happiness* by Michael Argyle.

De-stress yourself! Go for a relaxing massage that has many benefits besides easing tension from your stressed-out body! Here is what massage does for you, according to my amazingly talented massage therapist, Michelle Gallant.

"Massage affords us the opportunity to do just that—to just *be*. We spend so many of our waking hours doing, we become disconnected from ourselves. When receiving therapeutic massage on a regular basis, we are giving back to ourselves. We are creating an opportunity to receive, relax and allow. When we receive well-intentioned touch, the relaxation response takes place. Tissues within the body soften, creating a stronger flow of energy. As the body relaxes, the mind begins to slow down and thoughts begin to clear… allowing us to drop deeper into relaxation and begin to connect with our own essence, our highest self. Receiving massage on a regular basis allows us to get to this place of peace and clarity."

"The time to relax is when you don't have time for it."
–SYDNEY J. HARRIS

When I am run down from a crazy week or two, I can feel myself getting more tired than usual. Since I am naturally high-energy, my warning lights flash brightly when I observe these symptoms in myself:

>> Tired
>> Can't get out of bed
>> Need extra coffee to get moving
>> Not creative
>> Sore throat
>> Crankiness

Now that I am in tuned to myself, I halt all my usual routines and change my schedule so it includes NOTHING TO DO. I juice up on vitamin C and call in sick for work. This preventive method catches me up with myself and prevents colds and sickness. If I kept pushing myself when I feel my immunity already low, I would get a full-blown head cold and be out of work for four to five days. No thanks! I have more important things to do, and so do you.

The Brightest Warning Lights
Life is full of stress. Bad days will strike. They always do. It's life. No matter how much hand sanitizer you dish out, someone will get sick and have a fever, or be teething or have a bad dream, and you will be up all night. And those are the "good" bad days, with simple stressors that can be easily alleviated with some Tylenol or stuffed animals.

At some point, you will go through hell. Again, it's life. Horrible stuff happens to amazing people every day. As a social worker, mother, friend and woman, I've seen the awful things that can happen… illness, job loss, divorce, anxiety, death and disaster.

If you aren't prepared to cope with the daily stressors, when the big ones hit, you'll be wiped out. Dealing with the stress and chaos that children can bring to the family can also exacerbate any pre-existing conditions, like depression, anxiety, drug abuse and eating disorders. It is very important that you pay attention to your warning lights so you can catch something early, before you dive into a full-blown depression or need to get treatment for an eating disorder. This is wise and essential to your children's wellbeing.

I'm highlighting some important problems and their warning signs because it is happening all around us. If it's not you, it could be your neighbor or a mother from your son's classroom. These are not issues that affect only the mothers on the Doctor Phil television show. It is so imperative we know the signs and symptoms of serious problems before it is too late.

I have witnessed intoxicated mothers driving to pick up their children at school and I have stood by watching a mother starve herself for months to get into those skinny jeans. After working in the hospital emergency room as Director of the Crisis Team for over seven years, I have seen and heard it all. Many women try to cover it up, because they feel ashamed or embarrassed. Ladies, there is help out there for you. Please don't ever feel not worthy of help for fear of judgment about your mothering ability. **Even the best mothers have issues they need to work out**. Getting help is a gift you give yourself and those who love you. Plus, once you receive the help, it is confidential. They don't call your kid's school and announce it over the intercom, or put it on a billboard on the highway.

Psychotherapy gives women, who rarely have their own space, a special place of their own, according to my dear friend and psychologist Martha Bitsberger, Ph.D. In therapy, women learn how to accept and deal with their childhood issues, especially if the family of origin wasn't attentive, if there was a tragedy, or the family was plagued by alcoholism. Psychotherapy helps women be more comfortable in their own skin.

There are additional benefits to psychotherapy. One is being able to deal with a range of feelings. Martha says she often finds that many women are not able to deal with anger or sadness very well, but through the therapy process all of this comes to light, with the end result of women living more fully. You can gain a perspective on your childhood, your relationships and your parenting style as it relates to all of the above.

In the back of the book I have included a list of resources if you or someone you know is struggling with serious issues that can jeopardize joy and overall health. Please take the time to review this information if you are suffering or someone you know is in trouble. Please don't suffer alone. There are many places to get help.

The reason I've included information on these troubling issues in a book about reclaiming joy is simple. How do you find a deep joy when stress is a dark shadow over your life? Stress about money, employment, children, parents, the economy—it's everywhere and chances are you will experience different stress according to where you are in your life. I can't emphasize enough that it is imperative that you deal with stress in healthy ways. Walking around like a stress time bomb soaked with extra caffeine and sugar will take a devastating toll on your wellbeing, your health and your life. In the next chapter, we'll learn about resilience, which is pivotal in the making of a strong, confident, stress-resistant woman. If you want to learn to effectively manage your stress, resilience will pave the way.

CHAPTER 4

A Resilient Mother is the Best Mother

Resilient: Tending to recover from, or adjust easily, to misfortune or change.

M otherhood brings you the daily stressors and life throws you curveballs infused with pain and heartbreak. You can't go down with the ship, ladies. What can you do? You find your inner strength and deal with what comes. Of course, I am assuming you have inner strength. You see, inner strength is not something you are just born with. Resilience comes from a mix of having psychologically sound parents, faith in yourself and perhaps a higher power, dedication to healthy practices, and some great friends.

I can tell just by meeting people what their resilience level is and whether they are working from an increased level of strength or plummeting levels. I can know just by a brief conversation if what you do in your waking hours will add to your resilience or take it away. It is not one particular factor that makes you strong, it is many factors and it takes a fair amount of work to get there. Once you have resilience it takes effort to maintain it. It's worth every bit of energy you put into creating a strong you. No one else can do the work for you.

Resilience is something you work on every day. Someday when something difficult has happened, don't believe that you will wake up resilient after years of not taking care of yourself. It doesn't work that way. You're more likely to find yourself on the couch, crying, not wanting or able to deal with it.

Jane grew up in a large family where she watched her father drink himself to sleep every night. Her mother worked long hours and lacked a compassionate touch. They were nice parents, never yelled or hit, but never gave the children any inner substance.

The kids were left to fend for themselves for any nourishment and praise they could find. They would often find themselves only half-finishing everything they started, and as adults were plagued by addiction, divorce and low self-esteem. Every time life was tough, the siblings would reach for drugs, quit their jobs and end their relationships. Jane and her sisters had no sense of resilience. Jane had lost the ability to compensate when bad luck struck and couldn't seem to reach for anything positive.

Research by the Virginia Resilience Project has shown that the key elements in building resilience are:

1. healthy coping
2. self-knowledge
3. personal meaning and perspective
4. optimism
5. healthy relationships

Because resilience is such a big factor in your joy level, let's look at these five key resilience building blocks, one by one.

Healthy Coping

How do you cope when bad events occur or when life throws you a curveball? Do you grab hold of your faith and pray? Do you grab a bottle of alcohol or pills? Do you call your best friend and have a good cry? Do you start your therapy sessions again? Do you call out sick for two weeks and lie in bed like a zombie?

Your coping style says a lot about you. Healthy coping like therapy, prayer, exercise, friends, and/or support groups all suggest a strong person in need of some help through a tough time. If we are healthy, we give our children healthy ways to cope when they lose first place to their best friend in the science fair, when they break up with their boyfriends/girlfriends, when they don't make the baseball team, or when they don't get asked to the prom.

journal entry

Coping Skills

What do your coping strategies look like?

_____

_____

_____

_____

Think about this for a moment: How do you cope?

_____

_____

_____

_____

_____

How did your parents cope? How does your spouse cope?

_____

_____

_____

What are some coping skills that get you through hard times? Are these coping skills healthy or unhealthy?

_____

_____

Self-Knowledge

Know thyself! How do you do that? Through silence and solitude.

It's true, in this busy, media-rich world of ours, we need to silence our minds and our surroundings if we hope to hear our inner voice. We won't hear it any other way. Why is it that everywhere we go, the music is playing, the televisions are on… and that is just in the elevator going down one floor! Is all that noise necessary? How can we hear what is really going on inside us if we are not still? A beautiful book, *Intimacy and Solitude*, by Stephanie Dowrick, makes excellent points about what solitude offers you:

The chance to go back into myself to renew myself
The chance to check out what I am thinking and feeling
The chance to drift and dream and think at my own pace
The chance to cease to be attentive to the needs and demands of others

My favorite line is the last one. When you have children, you stand at attention to the needs and demands of others at all times. Imagine taking a break from that! You not only need it, you *deserve* it. When there are tough questions in your mind needing well-thought-out answers, being alone is the only way. Here is my friend Myra's story:

Myra had been in a relationship with a man she loved for over 25 years. She loved him but she thinks she might have outgrown him somewhere around their fifteenth year together. She tried her best to stay happy and appreciate him, partly because they had children to raise together and partly because she never allowed herself a moment of quiet to actually think about the alternatives and question whether she was truly happy. Once her children went to college, Myra began seeking advice from her friends on what she should do. Her friends encouraged her to take some time for herself, because this was not a decision they could make for her. This would be a huge, life-changing decision that needed to come from her own heart and soul. She booked a vacation to a yoga retreat center and spent two weeks praying and soul-searching. The answer was ready for her once she took that quiet time. She realized that she no longer felt satisfied in her relationship, and that she needed to leave. Despite the tears and pain, it was the right decision for her.

"If you wanna fly, you got to give up the shit that weighs you down."
–TONI MORRISON

Personal Meaning and Perspective

What gives meaning to your life? What do you do for work? Is it in line with your belief system?

Keeping things in perspective reminds me of this quote below:

"The beautiful thing about the human condition is that what looks like the end of the road never is. It is only the end of the road we know." (*The Joy of Burnout*, Dr. Dina Glouberman)

Do you flip out and lose it over little issues? When your kid flunks his spelling test, one out of the forty he's passed, do you lose your mind? Or can you keep perspective? When your little one spills the apple juice, can you keep the perspective that she is only twelve months old and that it is normal for little ones to spill things? She didn't do it on purpose to annoy you (one can never tell, but indulge me in this one).

Keeping a healthy perspective is a challenge when you don't take care of yourself. Let's think again about the road rage guy who gets out of his car ready to knife another driver over what he thinks was someone cutting him off in traffic. Do you think this guy has a clear perspective on life?

When your mind is full of all the chores, activities, stressors, bills and deadlines in your life, it is very hard to see through a clear lens. You tend to blow up at the little stuff or believe the world is ending when your son forgot his homework at school.

Not sleeping well can also contribute to a loss of perspective. How can you see the larger picture when you haven't slept or afforded yourself some much-needed down time? Walking around tense all the time in no way puts you in a position to handle your life well. As we learned in Chapter 3, filling your body with extra caffeine and junk food further weakens you. Yes, there's a theme here. Your healthy perspective gets swept away when you are not taking care of yourself in mind, body and spirit. You must choose to have enough sleep, exercise and good nutrition. Coffee is fine in moderation but it's not a substitute for sleep.

Building Resilience in Children

It is your responsibility to build resilience in your children. It is not the job of your children's school nor the Sunday school nor the Boy Scouts or the Girl Scouts. These are all great building blocks to add to your child's life, but it is your job as a parent to build your kid's self-esteem, self-awareness and coping mechanisms. It is your responsibility to give your kids *substance*. Spoiling them with material wealth and objects and urging them to try to be better than others is not substance. Spoiled kids crumble and turn to unhealthy coping skills when the going gets tough. Belittling and demeaning your children, calling them names and insulting them is not healthy parenting and builds a child with enough issues to last a lifetime. When you devote quality time to building your own resilience, it will reflect onto your children.

Don't seek to surround your child in a safe cocoon without any tough experiences. I know it is hard to watch a child who didn't make the soccer team, or who was just dumped by her boyfriend, or whose play date just cancelled and is hysterical (four-year-olds look forward to their play dates!). Some difficulty is part of life. Although we never want our children to feel pain, these are teachable moments in which you can help them gain resilience. Let them cry and feel disappointment. Give them space to scream and feel angry. Don't try to make it all better. Allow them to feel these uneasy feelings. This is where growth and character-building happen.

How does a parent with no coping skills and low resilience pass high resilience to their children? They don't. Plain and simple. Your kids watch how you cope with life. They are like sponges—even when you think they are not looking, be assured that they are indeed. They notice you grab the cigarettes, the drugs, the alcohol, the pills, the junk food, and they feel you become irritable, angry and sullen. When a parent walks into the home stressed and snapping at everyone, the energy and the mood takes a negative shift. You are responsible for the energy you bring to your home.

Children see and feel how you respond to the tribulations of life. They are perceptive little people who hear, see and feel everything. They can even sense our moods in the womb. All the more reason for us to be resilient and to take care of ourselves.

Pay close attention to what you watch on television. Are the shows sending you positive vibes or negative ones? There are plenty of reality shows that give you an hour of tension, anger and dysfunction. Is that how you want to spend your time? Are you allowing those nasty people into your living room or bedroom? Watching the news (which I refer to as the "bad news") can bring you everyone who has been shot, killed and raped all before you even start your day. What a downer to fill your being with such a wave of sadness! You can also go to sleep after a hard day, tired and, courtesy of the nightly bad news, also filled with fear. (Don't leave your home, bed bugs! Don't eat that, it causes cancer! Be careful about that, not safe!)

What does this have to do with joy? You may be unaware that your mood is affected by the media you consume. Watching nasty, irritating, self-absorbed people on your television screen might leave you with a warped sense of the human race. Listening to the bad news, morning or night, can suck the joy right out of you. I am not saying you have to be ignorant of or oblivious to the world's current events. By all means, be a knowledgeable and caring person, just watch how and when you are getting your news. Remember, there is plenty of good in the world, it is just not what the media wants you to hear and see. They want to grab your attention with negative, frightening, horrific news. Don't get sucked into it. Stay focused on your own joy.

Optimism and Humor

When my bad days strike, I focus on the saying, "This too shall pass."

When my daughter suddenly developed night terrors and changed her sleeping pattern to be up at least three times a night for four months, I hated everyone. I was a walking zombie, deprived of deep, refreshing sleep. I understood why sleep deprivation was an effective form of torture. It was probably the worst time in my life. I didn't want to be social, the holidays came and I pretended to smile, but even that was a stretch. I clung to my friends, who would hug me and tell me "This too shall pass." I had to believe them with all my heart because if I didn't, I would have left and never come home.

Then my daughter changed her pattern again and slept, and I slept, too. I loved my life again.

"And the Gold Goes to..."

If using every last ounce of energy you can possibly muster up to drag your overtired, sleep-deprived, cranky ass out of bed to get your kid to school on time was a sport, I so would've earned the gold medal today...and in an ideal world, I would've proudly accepted that sucker, climbed right back into my warm bed and slept like a baby until noon or so."

–WHERE'S THE FU*#KING MOMMY MANUAL?

Here is my friend Beth's story. Right after her divorce, Beth's son started having panic attacks before school every day. He wouldn't enter the school once the bell rang and he would cry and tantrum day after day. My friend went to the school meetings, the therapists, and did all that she could short of pulling her own hair out of her head. She had no choice but to homeschool him. Her spirit was heavy and her world was upside down. One day, she texted me, "I just don't know what to do anymore." I simply replied to her, "Don't worry, school sucks anyway." Her reply: "That's why I love you." She later told me that my simple text pulled her out of the darkness and gave her the strength to keep working. Months later, her son returned to school and her life resumed.

"Be with those who help your being."

—RUMI

Be an optimist. Envision solutions to problems and believe you can get through rough times.

"Optimists have a strength that allows them to interpret their setbacks as surmountable. Pessimists are eight times more likely to become depressed when bad events happen. They have worse physical health, shorter lives and rockier interpersonal relations." —from *Authentic Happiness*, Martin Seligman

When I met Angie she was settling into her new home life, beaming with joy. She shared with me the story of her most difficult move across the country. She was a stay-at-home mom with two small children, her husband had a great job and she had a beautiful home. She had plenty of friends, strong faith and a positive attitude. She never dreamed of what was to come. Her husband sank all of their money into a bad investment deal that landed them so far into debt that they lost their home and money in a matter of six weeks. They had to take what they could and move across the country from a small town in Rhode Island to a big city in Arizona where her brother agreed to fix up his basement so they had a place to live.

Not once did I hear Angie bad-mouth her husband. She stood by him as part of a team, determined to make this work. She described the strength she needed as she packed up all of her belongings, leaving some of the children's toys behind, and drove across the country to the unknown. She quickly found work, as did her husband, found good daycare and began her new life. She prayed for strength and courage to start anew and allow her to leave the life she had known far behind. It would be five years before they were ready and able to purchase a home.

As you read her story, some of you will think, "That's what women do, hold up the world, I would do the same." That is the resilience in you. Not all women have that resilience. Not all women can pick up the pieces when life goes bad and create a new life. Angie was resilient, her children saw a strong mother embrace the changes without skipping a beat. Did she cry in the privacy of her bedroom? Enough to fill a small lake. But she got up every day ready to take on the challenges, stay optimistic and know it would all work out. And it did.

Optimism

How do you view the world? Through a lens of glass half-full or glass half-empty?

Are you naturally optimistic?

Do you interpret your setbacks as surmountable?

Researchers are finding that even the slightest bit of optimistic attitude will serve you better in life than pessimism. Optimists even live longer!

According to Martin Seligman,

"When we are in a positive mood:
  • *people like us better, and*
  • *friendship, love, and coalitions are more likely to cement.*
In contrast to the constrictions of negative emotion, our mental set is
expansive, tolerant, and creative.
We are open to new ideas and new experience."

Wow! Amazing! What three words could be better to have when you are raising children? Expansive. Tolerant. Creative. Yes! Building your resilience and being open to new ideas and new experiences.

There are times when you just have to laugh! Laugh loudly, laugh to yourself, laugh until you pee your pants, *just laugh*! Laugh at how silly your daughter looks trying to impersonate Katy Perry. Laugh at how your son thinks his wand will really turn him into something from Harry Potter (even though you wish he would point it your way and magically land you on a Caribbean island with the Abercrombie and Fitch model whose muscled stomach makes you want to reach for your vibrator—you know who I am talking about, his photo is on the shopping bag). Laugh at how your son gets ready for his date with too much cologne. Laugh at how pathetic you are, you just paid for your medium coffee with dimes because all your dollar bills went to paying for that dumb library book the school said you lost. Yup, the last one was mine and I *laughed and laughed.*

Healthy Relationships and Good Friends

How do you feel when you spend an hour with women who are complainers, negative and unable to take good advice?

How do you feel when you are in the company of positive, uplifting women who want to learn and grow?

How would you rather feel?

Annoyed, frustrated, depleted, tired and worn out or joyful, excited and inspired?

You become the company you keep. Take a good hard look at who you're spending your time with. How do you feel when you leave them?

"People in supportive, loving relationships are more likely to feel healthy, happy, and satisfied with their lives."

—VIRGINIA RESILIENCE PROJECT

Your time is too precious for you to spend it getting the life sucked out of you. Spend it with friends who uplift and ignite your spirit. My friend Todd Patkin, author of *Finding Happiness*, encourages you to take a look at the people you regularly interact with and ask, *Are these people helping or hurting my quest for happiness*?

Take social inventory. Just because "negative Nellie" was a childhood friend doesn't mean you still have to be her friend. We all change and move in different directions as we age. Some people haven't changed one bit from high school, and I don't mean their appearance. Still gossiping, still high-drama, *ugh*! Who has the patience for that in their lives? I want to be in a no-drama zone! I only have friends who are true, trustworthy and genuine. So should you. You can have many acquaintances, as we do on Facebook, but would you really hang out with more than half of those people?

I know I say this as if it is easy, but for many of us it is a struggle. You may know your friend brings you down, but since you have been friends since childhood it is hard to not answer the phone when she calls to tell you about all her constant problems. It's okay to enact a slow, gradual release of the friendship. It doesn't have to be abrupt and rude. You may just to choose to see her once in a long while instead of every week.

Choose your friends wisely. When you have good close friends beside you, anything is possible. They are your cheerleaders, confidantes and best companions.

journal entry
Friends

Who are your good friends?

How would you describe them?

Do you need to do some weeding in the friendship garden?

Who might you think of letting go and why?

Your social circle is crucial for getting through rough times. You can't expect solid advice from people who don't take care of themselves and are not resilient. You will only get further frustrated. Remember that like attracts like. Look at the mothers in the schoolyard. Those who are confident and genuine do not surround themselves with the gossipy complainers. The benefits of a solid friendship are many. It is a true gift when you have found loving, non-judgmental friends. You will receive guidance when you most need it, a shoulder to cry on when you have had enough, encouragement when you are starting a new career, and unwavering love and support.

After a night of laughing with my friends, I feel nourished and full. I can't wait to be with them again. Some of our favorite nights are when we have a few couples over to play some fun board games. The night offers a ton of laughing, talking and sharing. It's inexpensive and the good feeling it promotes lasts for weeks.

Notice I didn't say, we have friends over and feel exhausted and depleted when they leave from hearing them bicker with each other, enduring their complaints that nothing ever goes right for them (when they are their own worst enemy) and listening to their laundry list of woes. Nope, I don't hang out with those people. I truly support my friends when they are at a life crossroads or dealing with tough stuff, but the constant negative complainers are not worth my time. Or yours.

"While income is not highly correlated with happiness and resiliency, researchers have found that social relationships are. This is very good news. People who are low on the happiness scale (perhaps due to genetically acquired gloominess) can raise their level significantly by closely interacting with a good friend on a daily basis." (Diener and Biswas-Diener, *Happiness*)

Create your social circle to be supportive and authentic. Open yourself to the experience of meeting new people. When you go to events at your child's school, spend time talking to the other mothers; you never know, the woman sitting next to you at the spring concert could be your next best friend. The three moms I met at my son's preschool over four years ago are still my close friends. How did I know when I brought my son to this preschool that I would be meeting my best friend? I didn't.

The friendship was a gift I received because I open myself up to new experiences in meeting new people.

I went out of my way to introduce myself and ask if we could get together for a play date. When you do that, you find out whether you click with someone or you don't. After a few hours together, you will know if this is a person you want as a friend. It is important to have at least two to four people close enough to count on when you need them, especially if you have no family help.

Don't parent in isolation. Your thinking can get rigid and you believe your way is the only way. There is a huge spectrum of healthy parenting. Some parents choose to be more strict and others looser. When you believe your way is the only way, you lose the potential to be open to new experience.

When parents get together to share their stories it is both comforting and informative. "You do that too?" "Oh, I never thought of doing it that way!" "Try this method." "Don't waste your time buying that, it doesn't work."

At one point, I was having a heck of a time every morning getting my son to wear a long-sleeve shirt in winter. He just loved short sleeves and never felt cold. So we battled every morning, until I spoke with some other mothers who completely normalized his preference for me. Their kids wore short sleeves always, as long as they either wore long sleeves over the T shirt or a jacket until they went into school. That was so interesting and very helpful to me. I tried this tactic and now we have no more battles over sleeves. I can say, "wear the short sleeves and enjoy your day."

"Life shrinks or expands in proportion to one's courage."
—ANAÏS NIN

52

Resilience and Self-Care Protocol

"Resilient people confront life's obstacles and emerge with greater wisdom, flexibility, and strength." –Virginia Resilience Project

What is your definition of resilient?

_____

_____

_____

_____

Are you a resilient person? Do you bounce back after difficult, challenging times?

_____

_____

_____

_____

_____

How can you build and maintain your strong resilience?

_____

_____

_____

_____

Did you grow up in a resilient family?

_____

_____

journal entry

Resilience and Self-Care Protocol (continued)

What are some qualities you have taken with you from your childhood to keep you resilient? (For example, perhaps your father was courageous or your mother always cooked healthy food, or sleep was valued as highly important, or your grandmother surrounded herself with devoted friends.)

_____

_____

_____

_____

_____

What qualities shown by adults from your childhood did you happily give up when you became an adult?

_____

_____

_____

_____

_____

What do you need to work on to stay resilient?

_____

_____

_____

_____

_____

_____

Although I mentioned exercise in Chapter 3, I wanted to mention it here, too. A resilient person is one who takes care of themselves in all areas of their lives, including physically. Exercise is key to stress release and overall health. Here are some other benefits of exercise, just in case you still don't believe me! Exercising does the following:

>> Releases endorphins in your bloodstream, creating a sense of well-being

>> Decreases muscle tension

>> Rids your body of toxins

>> Increases alpha wave activity in the brain, allowing you to clear your mind

>> Strengthens your heart and lungs

>> Helps you feel great in your body!

Remember, giving up is easy. Lying in bed all day crying is easy. Resilience takes work. **Self-care takes work.**

"If Joan of Arc could turn the tide of an entire war before her eighteenth birthday, you can get out of bed."

–E. JEAN CARROLL

When you have children, carving out that time for you feels unimportant. In fact, it is the most important thing you can do for your resilience and your joy. Who else will take care of you? Hold true to yourself and what nourishes you. Put back what you give out every day! When you have a great day, focus on what happened and why it was so good. Want it for yourself the following day. Don't stay focused on the negatives. Don't focus on what doesn't bring you happiness; put your energy into replicating the good days.

We offer great advice to others on how they can relax and de-stress, but can you take your own advice?

What is on your self-care list?

What makes you feel better when you have had a difficult day?

What can you do after a long weekend of being an attentive mother?

When do you reach your limit?

When have you just had enough?

I hit my limit every Sunday night around six-thirty. I just cannot hear "Mom, can I have…?" one more time without losing my cool. And you? How many questions like "Mom, can I have this? Mom, where are my sneakers? Mom, I'm hungry! Mom, can I have money? Mom, there's nothing in the fridge to eat!" can you tolerate before you begin to feel that your body is full of annoyance and frustration?

That's when your self-care protocol comes into play, your list to remind you of what brings you joy. What can you do to have a spectacular week? What can you put into your day and evening that brings you into a relaxed mode? Below are some ideas for you; feel free to add your own.

Self-Care Protocol—What's on your list? How well do you take care of yourself?

>> Walk, hike, be in nature

>> Say NO more often

>> Exercise regularly

>> Turn off the television

>> Challenge yourself

>> Laugh more

>> Surround yourself with inspiring and positive people

>> Spend time alone in quiet reflection

>> Say YES to new experiences

>> Keep dreaming

>> When you have a great day or an amazing week, figure out what you did and repeat it!

>> Take risks

>> Give yourself permission to play

>> Get plenty of sleep

>> Find your faith
>> Ask for help
>> Eat healthy foods
Source: www.thejoysource.com

What do you need for self-care? There are times when we need a change of scenery to lift our spirits. You know, those days when you just can't bear to look at the inside of your home one more minute or you will burst. When routine has gotten the best of you, go to the place you long to be. Not where people tell you to go. Not to a place that is negative. Nor to a place that you leave feeling frustrated and unhappy. Is it solace you need? Go for a hike in the woods minus the iPod and cell phone. Just you and your thoughts. Go where you need to be. Go to that place of excitement, joy and happiness. Don't go because you feel intimidated or guilty. Go where your heart is telling you to go. For each one of us needing comfort and love, it is a different place. Walk in the woods. Laugh with friends. Share passion with your soul mate. Experience joy with your children. Have a deep conversation with God. Go where your soul aches to go. *Only you know that place.* Give yourself permission to go there. Wherever it is. Just go. You'll be more resilient and be better able to cope.

Resilience has many building blocks. Healthy coping takes effort, but the payoff is immeasurable. The inner strength will sustain you as you go through the ups and downs of life. Self-knowledge is a lifelong journey! Start now! Spend time pondering what is really important to you and what holds the most meaning for you. When you focus more on your internal world and building a solid core foundation, you will go through life with a completely different mindset. One of strength, courage and true woman-power.

Resilience helps you keep your perspective when your life becomes chaotic and you believe you have lost touch with what means the most in your life. Those amazing, supportive friends you make serve such a strong purpose for you. They keep you from falling, they touch the sky with you when you are elated; they laugh and act silly with you. Ultimately, you are responsible for your own resilience. Your children will thank you for being a strong role model for them. Do the work, be your best; your joy will overflow. In the next chapter, you'll see how your resilience will come into play when we talk about the guilt that mothers can have over a variety of child-related issues.

CHAPTER 5

Mommy Guilt and How to Let Go of It

"Mommy, where are you going on vacation?" "Far, far away my child," she replied, guilt-free and ready for an adventure that didn't involve sippy cups and tempter tantrums.

I've been taking no-kid vacations with my husband since our children were infants. We went away for four days when my daughter was five months old. She was a difficult baby and I felt I was heading toward a breakdown if I didn't get away. Club Med Bahamas, here we come for five relaxing nights.

I've been known to hire babysitters on weekends to help out even when I am home, or for evenings to go out with friends into Boston for laughs and great food. (It feels great to dress up sexy!)

I used full-day daycare until my children were old enough to go to school. I found the best daycare in the world, and it's a good thing—there is no way I would have been able to do all those creative projects with my children that I now have as treasured souvenirs.

I work full-time and love every minute of being a professional.

I travel often, taking many weekends away either scrapbooking or with my girlfriends, or taking time alone to offset my ordinary days.

My husband is away every other weekend in the winter to go snowmobiling with his buddies.

My first point? I take breaks from my family and I have happy, well-adjusted children. How do I measure that?

They are rarely sick and have no allergies. When they draw, they draw rainbows and happy places with bright and vibrant colors. They have many friends and get good grades. They are positive and play outside every day (even in the summer rain). They sing prayers with me at night.

Are they perfect little angels and do I never want to scream? Of course not. That is why I am writing this book.

My second point is that you don't want to let "society" dictate to you what a "perfect" mother is and how she "should" act. You decide that. By some measures, I have broken every "rule" about being a mother. These are the top five "guilts" I "should" be feeling—but I'm not. How many of these do you identify with?

1. Bottle Feeder Guilt

 I didn't breast-feed. "Well, that is just horrible," you may be thinking. Well, not really. What was horrible was how I felt when I attempted to do it… trapped, exposed, sore and stuck… I hated every minute of it. And I don't want to argue with lactation specialists, but if you are going to use the argument that my kids would be healthier if I had breast-fed, I can tell you they are rarely sick. They are healthy children. This choice might not be for everyone, but it worked out fine for me and my children.

The important thing is to do what feels right for you. Some friends have said breast-feeding was the most beautiful time with their baby and I love hearing that. How wonderful for them! It just wasn't for me. I didn't want to be the only one who had to wake up and do all the feedings. Sorry kids, Mommy needs her sleep or she won't be very pleasant in the morning. Daddy is more than capable of waking up and feeding baby, and that is exactly what he did.

If I had given in to the guilt, I would have been worn out, frustrated, resentful and angry. What would I have had left to give to my precious newborn if this was how I was feeling? If I had let the guilt get the best of me, my connectedness to my children and my husband would have been strained. Instead, sharing the work landed me more sleep and a better frame of mind.

2. Time as a Couple Guilt

Wouldn't it be healthier for a child to see their mother and father acting lovingly toward each other and going out on date nights so she will know what a healthy relationship is as she begins to date? Or are you grooming your daughter for a marriage that equals "when you are married you give up everything you love to do, only focus on the children and also forget about your husband." Is that what you want to model for your child? Set a positive example.

Date nights are great, but vacations are even better! Taking adults-only vacations together and leaving our children with their grandparents was important to our relationship as a couple, and also gave my children a chance to enjoy their grandparents. I grew up spending weeks with my own grandparents as my parents needed their time to travel. I loved every second of it. They had a beautiful cottage on a lake and we swam and ran through the forest all summer long. Even now, as an adult, when I need a "happy place" to go back to in my mind, I close my eyes and think of those days with my cousin, swimming in the lake. My nana, making chicken noodle soup and grilled cheese. There was no television or phones, just a lot of nature and a lot of love. If my parents had not been able to leave us with others without feeling guilty, I would never have had those memories that still serve me so well today. If my parents hung around with people who pressured them *not* to ever leave their kids, they might have acted differently.

3. The Not a Stay-at-Home-Mom Guilt

I love working at my job and in my profession. I am using my talents and my gifts and I am authentically me. It feels great. And you? Are you currently in a profession where you are using your talents? There is so much research that supports the idea of finding what you love to do in your life and then doing it! It makes for a happier person!

I hear so many women say they are giving up something or "sacrificing" for their kids. Why? So you sacrifice your happiness and somehow that is okay? Do you truly believe that your children won't pick up on the fact that you passively feel resentful and annoyed that your hubby gets to escape every day and you are home changing diapers, dealing with temper tantrums and wiping noses?

If working makes you happy, then work even if it means you are netting less money because you have to put your kids in daycare. Do it anyway. You may feel that you need to have a purpose outside the home, and to have a place that is "yours." I don't mean volunteer at your kid's school. So many stay-at-home mothers tell me, "I volunteer at my kid's school." That's admirable, but it's good to also do something that doesn't involve your children. Replenish yourself and be ready for them when the school bell rings in the afternoon.

C'mon ladies! Find what makes your heart sing and your soul dance, find your purpose and find a way to bring that into your world. Even if it means putting your kids in a daycare for a few hours per day. Let the guilt go.

4. The Daycare Guilt

 I felt bad as my son cried when I left him at daycare. But guess what? He stopped crying the minute after I left and enjoyed his time there. I found a quality daycare and feel forever indebted to them. Robin was and still is an amazing women who runs an even more amazing daycare. She and her staff loved and hugged my children each day they were there.

My son always cried when I left him, and I may have appeared to be a cold-hearted mom as I turned and walked out the door. I am certainly not. It bothered me when I saw him crying at the door for me, but I also knew when I called back an hour later to check on him, he would be happier than ever. My daughter loved the daycare so much that when I would go in to pick her up she would make me wait as she hugged each of her classmates and then her teacher goodbye.

Could I have given them that same positive experience being at home with them all that time, hour after hour? No way! And no guilt felt here.

My children were much better off in this daycare than they were with me being a stay-at-home mom. My patience is limited and I am insightful enough to know that. I don't pretend to enjoy being home with my children for extended lengths of time, knowing that I max out after five or six hours. I know my limits—you should know yours, too.

5. Going Away Guilt

 "Mom, you're leaving for five days?" Yes, and I promise you I will come back a better person.

Go away. Far away or close by—just go. Enjoy a night out with your friends or just by yourself. Give yourself permission to leave and rejuvenate so you enter back into your world a better person. Your world will still be there when you get back. The kids will be screaming, clothes will be on the floor and the dishwasher will be ready to be emptied. So why not take a much-needed break?

If your excuse for staying home is that your husband won't know what to do, go anyway. He'll figure it out. My husband did. He bathes the children, knows exactly where my daughter's hair detangler spray is and will sit with her on the couch combing her hair. If she were a cat she would purr. He figured out the hair care routine and now it's a special time between the two of them.

Remember the team concept? A team works because everyone works together. What do you want your kids to learn about parenting as they grow older? That mothers do everything at home and fathers go out to work? That wouldn't get me excited about becoming a mother.

Don't give fathers the easy way out, because it ends up being exactly the opposite, the not-so-easy way out. The burden is heavy and placed on you. You create the scenario of "he knows nothing and you know everything." Which means you can't leave with peace of mind because he doesn't know where the kids' socks are and can't find the sneakers. The best thing about this situation is that since you created it, you can uncreate it. You can craft a new scenario where he has to figure out his own way of doing things. I promise, the kids won't get sick from frozen pizza two nights in a row.

When you go away and give yourself a change of scenery, you allow time to be yourself again. Just you. Not someone answering to others and caring for others. When you go away, shut the hotel door and do your happy dance. It's just you.

It is important to make someone happy. Start with yourself.

Guilt doesn't just come from inside us, it is imposed on us by others as well. Women have told me horrible stories of relatives, especially their own parents, placing heavy loads of guilt on them. The world is a changed place from 60 years ago. It is more complicated, moves faster and many women have careers. Don't take this guilt to heart and don't allow it to penetrate your being. When we feel guilty, we try to please others by shying away from what we really want to do. You have to stay true to yourself and what you need, not what others "think" you need.

See what you can learn from the story of a woman I met in my Joy Course, and then worked with in my joy coaching business. Jennifer tried to be a good daughter-in-law, doing everything she could to please her in-laws and relatives. She showed up at all the gatherings, allowed sleepovers and welcomed these people into her home at any time. After a while, she noticed that although she was doing all she could, it was never good enough for them. So she tried harder. She stayed all day at functions she never wanted to attend, carted her children around as her in-laws expected and still they had comments about how she was raising her children. Everywhere she turned was guilt, guilt and more guilt.

Jennifer's husband couldn't understand why she was so upset; he had lived with this his whole life so he didn't recognize it as wrong and hurtful. Jennifer thought it was just her and believed she would just have to live like this. She started to gain weight from the sadness of feeling "not good enough." Tension arose between her husband and herself, and she felt angry and resentful.

Jennifer's bright light was her support group. She had remained close to some childhood friends who became her lifeline. They would swap stories and offer support through her tears of frustration and sadness. All Jennifer knew was that things had to change. Her friends gave her the encouragement to seek professional help, with sessions that included her husband. She became a new woman by setting limits, saying "no," and by not taking relatives' comments so personally.

It is important to distinguish what is important to you and what is not. **What events and places bring you joy and which take from it?** When you go to a gathering or an event, whether alone or with your kids, pay attention to how you feel when you leave. Are you excited you just spent time with people you love? Or was it way too much work for you just to get there and emotionally draining for the duration? You have to be insightful and self-aware about what will make you happy and what will keep you grumbling. As you continue your emotional growth and grow older, this is a key piece to develop. Know what are good choices for you and how you spend your time. I can't emphasize this point enough! You want to get to a place in your life that despite the few places and obligations you cannot avoid, you spend your time in places with people who nourish you, excite you and fill you with happiness.

When my kids were very young, it only took me one graduation party for my husband's friend—who I didn't even know—to make me really sure I would never do that again. The party was not a good experience. A home full of people I didn't know, a baby who needed to be fed and changed, and a toddler who was drooling and touching everything and who we had to keep away from the long staircase for three endless hours. I was exhausted and so utterly annoyed at my choice to attend. It always sounded so great. "Oh, bring the kids, we would love to see them." You hear this all the time when your children are young. There were many times I could predict the amount of work I'd have to do to attend and see how it would not be a good time, so I would just say "no." I would rather be annoyed and frustrated in my own home with my own stuff to keep my kids occupied. This is where knowing yourself comes into play. If you are busy running around saying "yes" to every party, volunteering, extra work shifts... how do you know what brings you joy and what doesn't? Strive to be at a place of confidence in your life where you know what you love and where you want to be, and you *get there* as much as possible.

If you have Mommy Guilt, what are you going to do about it?

Perhaps there's another useful lesson from another woman from my joy coaching practice. Kara was born to be a mother. Caring, loving and very sensitive, she couldn't wait to be married and have many children. When she had her first little girl, Amy, she became consumed with her. She quit her job, gained weight, and alienated her husband from participating in any tasks associated with Amy because she wanted to be connected with her in any and every way possible. As Amy got older, Kara encouraged the child to sleep in the same bed with her, further alienating her husband by sending him to a couch in the living room. To Kara, "what's best" for her child meant never using babysitters and never going out as a couple with her husband. All that was gone once the baby entered the picture.

Talking with Kara, I discovered and she realized that her own childhood had been marked by loneliness. Her single mother was always busy and had a number of boyfriends. Kara came second or third to all of this. Every day after school Kara was home alone, a typical latchkey kid. Weekends were spent focused on her mother and Kara got lost in the shuffle. So when she had her own child, Kara devoted herself to making sure her daughter never questioned her mother's devotion and attention. And Kara got lost in the process.

Kara didn't realize how these feelings stay harbored inside unless you bring them to the surface to deal with them. This is why I highly recommend therapy, ladies! It is truly a gift you give to yourself.

Therapy helped Kara bring these painful memories to light and allowed her to work on them so she could give her husband some much-needed attention without feeling guilty about taking some attention from Amy. Because her own mother hadn't been there for her, Kara felt like every waking minute, and sleeping moments too, for that matter, had to be spent with Amy or she would be consumed by guilt. She didn't want Amy to grow up lonely, as she did. It all made sense, but it wasn't a healthy way to live.

Some of us have extreme guilt feelings, while others struggle with taking a night out now and then to rejuvenate. We may think "he can't go to sleep without me reading a book to him." Wanna bet?

journal entry
Mommy Guilt

Do you have any mommy guilt?

_____

Is this a feeling you placed on yourself or is it caused by someone else (family, culture, society)?

_____

_____

How does this guilt hold you back from a joyful life?

_____

_____

_____

_____

_____

_____

_____

_____

Mommy Guilt (continued)

Have you ever talked about the guilt you feel?

_____

_____

What have you done to work on releasing it?

_____

_____

_____

_____

_____

After reading this chapter, what are some steps you might take in order to let the Mommy Guilt go?

_____

_____

_____

_____

_____

_____

_____

Who Makes You Feel Guilty?

Who is it in your life who makes you feel guilty or triggers guilty feelings in you? Your parents? Your friends? Your in-laws? Society? Do you put that pressure on yourself to be the "Perfect Mother"?

I can't tell you how many spouses I've spoken to who say they encourage their wife to play more, to put the kids in daycare, get babysitters, lighten the load a bit, and the mothers just can't do it. They place unnecessary guilt upon themselves or allow their kids to guilt them.

Again, not every one of the options I mentioned above is right for everyone. Using daycare isn't a choice or an option for all mothers, I completely understand that. However, a balance of adult time and kid time is necessary for all! So figure out a way to get it!

Is it your kid you are responding to? A little one who cries when you leave? A school-aged child who wears a frown when he knows you are leaving for the night? A tween who yells and complains you are "always leaving her" (when you know that isn't true)? A teenager whose life you are "ruining" because you can't drive her to her friend's house if you go on your favorite scrapbooking weekend?

Children at any age, some aware of their behavior and others not, can send you into a guilt-ridden frenzy in no time. Don't give in! You will set yourself up for a lifetime of obeying your children instead of them obeying you! Give your children the message that mothers need their time to play, too. Mothers have friends to meet with, exercise classes to take and weekend trips or evenings out to have fun.

Moms Just Want to Have Fun

Give yourself the ability to experience pleasure, whatever that means for you.

Why should kids have all the fun? You deserve to have fun, too. You are worthy, you are the mother, and if you are not happy, who is?

When your life is moving at a fast pace, take a sick day from work. You don't have to be sick to take a mental health day. You are taking care of yourself, which makes you a better employee. Look at it this way, you are actually doing your colleagues and your boss a favor.

My own research with the many women I speak with daily reveals that they are the happiest and most productive when they are taking care of themselves, balancing the work and the play.

>> Sit on the couch and have a leisurely cup of coffee or tea.

>> Watch a movie at home or go out to a movie.

>> Take yourself out for a delicious lunch and then get your nails done.

>> Get to that exercise class you have been meaning to try and then relax in the steam room after.

>> Walk around the mall, window-shop or buy yourself some new clothes.

>> Go for a hike, find tranquility in nature.

journal entry

A Day for You

Imagine that you have the entire day off, no kids, no responsibilities, no work. How would you spend such a day? Be specific. I want you to imagine what will you be doing or not doing each and every hour of that day.

Before 9 a.m.

9 a.m.

10 a.m.

11 a.m.

12 p.m.

journal entry

1 p.m.

2 p.m.

3 p.m.

4 p.m.

After 4 p.m.

Reflection: When was the last time you had a day like this?

Is this day actually possible in your life right now?

Why or why not?

How would you feel at the end of the above day?

Don't Let Guilt Sap Your Joy

Guilt can suck the joy out of your life, and your family's life, too. It can linger around you, in you and cause you to do things you don't want to do. It can certainly prevent you from having a joy-filled life. If you are someone who feels guilt for "not giving in to your kids" or "going out for a girls night," I urge you to address those feelings and get to the root of what they really mean. Your joy and your family's joy is at stake here! Read what my seven-year-old son wrote unsolicited.

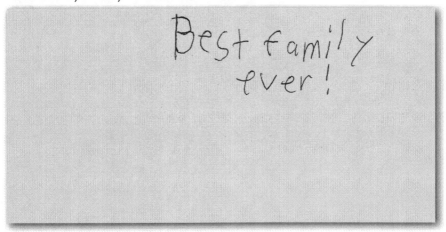

Would anyone in your family be likely to write a note that reflected a similar sentiment? Or would someone write "We never have any fun" or "Mommy's always mad"?

Guilt can hold you back from a joyful, authentically *"you"* life. Guilt can appear in our lives at different times for different reasons. You may have no idea where it came from and why it plays a huge part in your life. This is often the most difficult concept for women to wrap their heads around; saying YES to themselves and offering a kind NO to others. I encourage you to spend time thinking about how guilt plays a role in your life. Saying yes to everyone will deplete you of your energy and leave you no time for you. When you are giving of yourself without putting back what you gave, you are in danger of losing yourself to family (and/or others). The next chapter explains how that losing yourself happens and how to feel the triumph of taking yourself back to a joyful, delightful you.

CHAPTER 6

Losing Yourself to Family

"And while it's part of human kindness to want to please others, nothing is gained if we lose ourselves in the process."
—W. TIMOTHY GALLWEY, THE INNER GAME OF STRESS

....

R ead these two women's stories, and think about who you would rather be.

Alice chose to be a stay-at-home mom. She likes to be in control and manages the household finances, the schedules and everything in between. She laughs when people tell her she needs a break; they can't be referring to her, she does it all just fine. She loves being home and in charge of her world. What she hasn't noticed is how much she yells at her children, how she is so exhausted at the end of the day that she doesn't even notice her husband, and how during certain weeks she has had no adult contact except for the cashier at the supermarket checkout counter. She is too busy worrying about baths, homework and household chores to notice that her world has become very small. She often finds herself with little patience and snaps at her family over minor infractions.

Jill is a stay-at-home mom who could live in "mommy land." She loves doing art projects and playing dress-up, and she revels in every aspect of parenting. But she knew she needed a break when she started feeling resentful and angry that her spouse gets "adult time" in his job. When she tried to get a part-time job, a few evenings a week, she was unsuccessful. She couldn't wait for something to come along, because she knew she needed some adult time very soon. So she decided to volunteer teaching English as a Second Language two nights a week and a half-day on Saturday. This gave her the opportunity to completely miss the nightly household routine twice a week—no dinner, no dishes and no bath time. Jill felt like a new woman who had the best of both worlds. She had a purpose at home and in the adult world, and a break from "mommy land." A great side effect: on the nights when he is the man in charge, her husband gains a better appreciation of all that she does.

We can easily lose ourselves in the all-consuming state of motherhood, which is why I wrote this book. I have seen the whole spectrum, from mothers who work 60 hours a week to mothers who don't work any hours outside the home. Some women relish their roles as mothers while others despise the same roles. We are all different in our expectations, our needs and our wishes, except for our need for the one thing that matters so much: balance.

No matter what our choices are, balance must be on the top of our list. Why? We are happier and all parts of us are getting fed when we are full in body, mind and spirit. There are plenty of happy stay-at-home mothers who have a full range of hobbies, volunteer their time (beyond the school) and enjoy a close relationship with their husbands.

Such women have got it right. They have balance.

There are working mothers who pay babysitters and housecleaners so they too can have time off from chores and enjoy their free time. Balance is possible for them, too.

Don't Compare Yourself to the Glamorous Celebrity Moms

A side note… Do not compare yourself to the celebrity women who gush to the television talk show hosts and magazine interviewers, "Parenting is a dream, my child is perfect in every way, I enjoy every moment with her." These celebrity mothers often have nannies and a staff of assistants and stylists, have oodles of money and a different perspective on what most of us think of as "real life." Sometimes, watching these women can make you feel bad about your own life.

I was struck by how I felt one day after watching a talk show host interview a new Hollywood mother. The mother looked perfect in every way and spoke about motherhood as just perfect joy every day. I am not bashing her—if she feels joyful, that is wonderful. However, I couldn't help but think of all the mothers watching that same show who had been up all night with crying babies. Those moms no doubt had their bleary eyes half-open, their hair was a mess, and they were hanging on by a thread. How does watching that interview make them feel?

We are bombarded with these idealized and glamorized images of mothers everywhere. If you are feeling down about yourself, stay away from the talk shows and the celebrity magazines. Don't read the articles about Mrs. Famous Movie Star's body only three months after giving birth. Such articles are rarely realistic, and usually leave out details like the star has a workout facility in her home, a personal trainer who visits every day, a nanny who cares for her children and the money to pay for it all.

How does that compare to my life? I get to the gym, eyes half-open and wearing a cheap T-shirt from Target, at 5 a.m. because that is the only time I can fit it in my busy, not-so-glamorous schedule of work and chores. It took me one year after the birth of my child to get my body back. My doctor told me that it took nine months for my body to sustain the baby, and it will take you that long to get it back. Be patient with yourself if you are trying to get back into shape. It's worth the effort, but be realistic and kind to yourself.

Leave the unrealistic expectations in Hollywood, ladies, let them go. Focus on being the best woman you can be, don't compare yourself to anyone else but yourself. Be better than you were yesterday, that's all you need to worry about. Ask yourself: Am I growing and learning? Am I using all my gifts and talents?

A Note for Stay-at-Home Mothers

Before I had children, I thought being a stay-at-home mom was the best idea ever. I would see women with their kids at the mall and hope that I too would get that opportunity to spend the days loving and snuggling my children. Never missing a milestone, relishing their amazing developing personalities. And then came my children.

I tried desperately to enjoy the time off from work, but I couldn't help but envy (and get a little resentful of) my husband as he got ready and left every day to go out and work. Staying home all day with an infant, changing the diapers and doing the feedings… and changing diapers and feeding… was not for me. I tried all the mommy groups and couldn't stand any of them. How much can we stand around and only talk about our kids?

It took me a while to admit this to myself, because all the other women around me loved it. In fact, they loved it enough to quit their jobs and become totally immersed in "mommy land." I felt lost, and then I realized if I stayed too long in this place, I would lose myself completely.

So I went back to work and asked for even more hours so I could put my children in daycare. I even put them in daycare on my day off so I could also have a day off and enjoy my time without children (I know, insert awe and shock here).

I was desperate for that "me time," you know ME, the Julie I once was. I guess I didn't realize it was going to be a fight to put myself first. That I would have to work so hard to make sure I didn't lose myself, especially since putting myself first only meant nourishing myself in such a way that I felt happy and full for my children.

It is great if you enjoy being a stay-at-home mother. In fact, I know many women who feel it is a blessing. Great! Good for you. I just say, find a balance. Please stay connected to the outside world. I have spent countless hours with women who gave up careers and a strong sense of independence to stay home, and who are now regretting it.

If staying at home with your children is your preferred option, please stay connected to yourself by taking the time to do what you want to do. Don't think you are the only exception, the only mother who does not need a break. If you think that, your energy is directed in one place and one place only, your children. You have no balance, no sense of being full and complete. You have let go of your hobbies and your needs, and most likely are neglecting your spouse, too.

Lily loved her life before children; she had a great job, earned money, had her own bank account, met with friends after work, loved getting dressed up for work. She quit her job when the children came and her husband made it seem like it was a gift that she got to stay home. Little did she anticipate that seven years later she would be an empty shell of a woman. Her husband never stopped working, enjoys his pastimes and has never skipped a beat in his life. She is like a ghost in the home. She feels little purpose and each day blends into the next. She is bored and feels misled. No one warned her she would feel this way. Even beginning to get back into the workforce with low self-confidence feels like it will never happen for her. Lily often thinks to herself, if her husband left her, she would be left with nothing—no job, no career. She came to me for some joy coaching. In time, we worked together to get her back on a joyful track in her life, finding her purpose and having the courage to make positive changes.

Consider this your warning: Marriage and children can get the best of you if that is all you do, day after day. Remember my example about the airplane and the oxygen mask? Take a full, hearty breath before trying to help your children. Doing laundry and being a taxi driver will not keep you growing and being your best. Stay connected to the outside world! You know, the world you created for yourself as an independent woman, before you became a mother. It feels good to earn your own money, buy yourself little treats and save for your retirement. Feeling a sense of purpose goes hand-in-hand with feeling happiness. Giving it all up can also mean giving up your self-confidence and your purpose.

Being a mother is *one* part of your life, it is not everything or the only thing about you. What else are you capable of? Where else are your talents?

If you are a stay-at-home mom, here are some things you can do to keep focused on yourself:

 >> Keep a journal; write down your dreams and your hopes.
 >> Find time to read books (without pictures). Reading takes you away.
 >> When your children nap, throw on an exercise tape or DVD and work out. Don't do the laundry and chores. Do something for you. They told me in prenatal classes to nap when my baby napped, but I just wasn't a nap person. I chose to work out instead, and I felt great for the rest of the day. Consider investing in an elliptical machine if you can't join a gym to get a total body workout. If you do need naps, then definitely take them and use this time to refresh and rejuvenate.

>> Stay focused on healthy eating; don't eat a snack every time your child does.

>> Get a sitter if you can, even for just an hour or two a week.

>> Carve out nights that are for you. If you have a spouse, let him manage the child care and household duties a few nights a week; you leave as he comes home. I know so many women, who, before they go out, bathe the children, feed them and then leave! Why bother leaving? Miss the routine at least once per week. We all need a break and that includes you. Some of you are snickering reading this, saying "yeah, right." I'm telling you that you can't afford *not* to; otherwise you are at risk of falling into the trap of the same old routine, going on autopilot. Find a way to take a break.

My friend Kim was a stay-at-home mom with two boys. She enjoyed being home with them and was happy to give up working at a local retail store when her husband got a promotion. "There came a time when I just felt burnt out on being a mom," she told me. "I thought I could do everything and I felt like I hit a wall." Due to limited cash, she posted on her Facebook page about her idea to get more time for herself. She would watch her friends' children for two or three days per week for no more than three hours if they would return the favor. Other stay-at-home moms jumped on this idea, and soon she found it was sometimes easier to have other children around as playmates for her children, and she cherished the time to herself on her non-sitting days. "Sometimes I would just lie on the couch and watch a movie or take a long bath. I made a point to not fill up that time with chores." Smart woman. Don't fill up all of your "you" time with chores that don't give you much back. Instead, spend your time engaging in an activity or hobby that lets you feel refreshed and ready to take on the day.

A Note for Working Mothers

Mothers who work outside the home have different challenges than stay-at-home mothers, but they often feel it is worth it. There are some women with such demanding jobs that they are at the opposite end of the spectrum, where they are missing the school plays, the after-school programs and time with their children. It breaks my heart to see women who want to be home—or at least be more active at their kid's school—and who, because of their jobs, can *not* do it. Some have inflexible work environments where they can't leave early or in the middle of the day and others have long commutes; if this is you, hang in there. When you believe there are no other options, you feel sad and frustrated. Some are only "stuck" in a miserable situation for a few years, then they can make changes. Make every moment with your children count. Play often and creatively. Don't get down on yourself. Brainstorm with others (or me—that's why I have a joy coaching business) about what options may be out there to help make changes in your life that better suit you.

Ideally, part-time work is an option that allows for balance between work and children, but that's not always realistic. Not every mother wants to work outside the home. With the economy being what it is, choosing to work is often not optional; for some women it is the only option.

Secret Weapons for Not Getting Lost

I have five "secret weapons" to help you not get lost. They are:

1. Spend your time wisely.
2. Learn how to say no.
3. Beware the Martyrs and the Not-Worthy Women.
4. Sidestep the Joy Suckers.
5. Keep it real!

Let's go through them one by one.

1. Spend Your Time Wisely

One of the most important concepts for you to grasp so you don't lose yourself to your family is a simple one that applies to all mothers, whether working outside the home or not: spending your time wisely.

Some mothers are organizing champions, with to-do lists and chore charts, while other mothers wake up and take on the day without a plan or a prayer.

Ladies, don't waste your precious time and energy foolishly. Recently, my son's school library sent home a note that until he returns the book that was due four months ago, he could not take out another book. I did spend a few minutes looking through his bookcase, but couldn't find it. By accident, I probably donated it or it is somewhere in the 10 toy buckets around my home. Who knows? I certainly don't and neither does he. Will I spend three hours uncovering every toy-filled surface, spending my energy ripping up my house from top to bottom when I can just send in the $7.95 and pay for the lost book?

Where is your time better spent?

Do you create an overscheduled life for yourself and then complain? Do you fail to give your children household chores and then complain that you have to do everything? Do you not enforce the rules and then complain because no one follows them?

Make your life easier. Tell your children, "We all help out in this home, we are all a team." Give them chores so you don't have to do everything. Don't set yourself up for frustration and resentment. Create the world you want! It takes work, but it is worth it. Instead of spending three hours looking for a lost library book, I wrote a check and spent the three hours doing something I enjoyed.

My friend has a fifteen-year-old daughter who is not doing well in school. She and her husband have tried helping her with studying and homework, and someone always leaves the dining room table frustrated and swearing. She reports, "Everyone gets frustrated and my daughter isn't doing better academically." Her solution? Get the girl a private tutor. My friends says, and I quote, "If you can't fix the problem, pay someone else to." If money is an issue, be creative. For example, can you swap something you do well for a tutor's time?

Spend Your Time Wisely

Do you spend your time wisely?

Are you organized?

What chores take up most of your time?

Can you walk by the pile of laundry on the stairs to do what you want to do for 30 minutes?

If not, is this something you can commit to working on?

Taking time for you needs to be part of your day.
How will you do it going forward?

2. Learn How to Say No

 Let's face it, children deplete you! Mothering is emotionally and physically exhausting. And it's just not the constant direct demands from your children, but also from the rest of the strange world you are suddenly part of when you become a mother.

Have you ever noticed that once you had children, you were invited to a ton of parties? There are birthdays, communions, bat mitzvahs, holiday parties with Santa and the list goes on and on.

For some reason, your family members want you to "bring the kids" to these events, so you feel even more pressure to attend. Once upon a time, I gave in to these demands. I was invited to every party for every occasion for people I didn't even know and family members expected me to be there. I had no free time, and lugging little children around, missing their naps, and changing their diapers in hallways was not my idea of fun. I hated every minute of it. I complied until I couldn't take it anymore.

Then I did the most outrageous, most insane thing of all.

I started saying NO.

>> No, I can't attend that two-year-old's birthday party at Chuck E. Cheese in the middle of my son's nap time.

>> No, I can't attend that graduation party for a friend's daughter I don't even know.

>> No, sorry, that day I am busy.

>> No, no, no!

I only went to parties that I wanted to go to. Sometimes my husband took the kids without me and others we skipped out on entirely. I got smarter. I even pay the babysitter to take my children to parties when I need to get work done or I need an afternoon to myself. My children always have a great time. I don't need to be waiting on the sidelines of the loud funhouse in order for them to enjoy themselves. Yes, it would be great to see them jumping and having a great time, but we were just there last month.

My friend Clara just came back from a miserable Girl Scout outing where you sleep on the floor in a museum for the night. She had initially turned down the request, but felt the guilt vibes from her daughter looming in the air, as well as from the other mothers insisting she would have "fun." Clara knew it was not a good idea, because she needs sleep to function. She could predict fun during the day but a no-sleep night, and knew that working a full day the following day would be a disaster.

Against her better judgment, Clara finally gave in and decided to go. She didn't sleep even an hour, returned home to three children (no time for a nap!) and was a zombie the next morning for work. It wasn't worth it. She was frustrated about giving in to the guilt and not holding a firm no. My advice? You live and learn. We all do this and later struggle with why we said yes in the first place. Learn from these experiences. Don't keep saying yes and repeating what you already know was not good for you!

How do you know when you have had enough? Can you recall a time that you really wanted to say no but didn't? There are some parties that will be fun for everyone, you might see some good friends and share some laughs. There are others that will give you a headache and make you want to bang your head against the wall.

So give it a try and say no.

But here is the BIG catch and a huge warning about saying no and why women have a hard time enforcing their no's:

People will get angry at you.

You will probably upset some hosts/hostesses who will be hurt that you didn't come to their gathering. Other invitees will become annoyed that you are setting boundaries and they cannot. They feel they are stuck going, and you should be too.

I love this question from the writings of Oriah, who asks,

"Can you disappoint another to be true to yourself?"

Well ladies, can you? When you say no to a person who gets angry, can you sit with that anger? Or is it too painful for you, so you retreat and end up saying yes even though you don't want to? Can you sit with the disappointment of your friends and family members to stay true to yourself?

My best friend sent her husband to a gathering where he would say, "Sarah needs some time to herself, that is why she is not here." His family's reply was classic:

"It must be nice."

I remember how hurt I was once when we were planning a trip to Club Med, just my husband and I, so in need of time away. And when I told people, I got that same response: "It must be nice."

Or when I took a few hours off one afternoon and treated myself to a mani-pedi. "It must be nice."

When people say to you, "it must be nice," you almost feel like you need to defend why you are doing good things for yourself. At that point we start to second-guess ourselves. "Oh, should I not be doing this? Maybe I don't deserve to be happy and have time for myself."

This is where women can waver a bit and decide it is too painful to have people angry at them or make snide comments, so they decide it just isn't worth it. They will trudge along and find joy another time in their lives. Or they will question whether they are worthy. Do they deserve a break, time away for fun, moments of complete "selfishness"? Because that's what it begins to feel like… that horrid word, selfish… self-centered behavior, when really it's just about enjoying your life! But I tell you, the selfishness is not you… it's the women who can't allow others to have those moments of joy!

This is what happens when you hang out with the wrong people! Joyless, jealous people who want you to be as miserable as they are. You know those people… the crabby, complaining, rarely smiling mothers in the schoolyard who gripe about everything.

You need people in your life who say, yes, you deserve that vacation. Yes! You are so in need of time to yourself, good for you for getting a sitter. Yes! You are deserving of the good life! YES! When we begin to defend ourselves, it feels crappy. Do I really need to defend why I need time alone? No, I don't, and neither do you. Ladies, when people say to you "IT MUST BE NICE," please don't ever defend yourself. Simply reply,

"YES, IT IS."

3. Beware the Martyrs and the Not-Worthy Women

 Let me explain the two types of people who might make you feel like you need to defend yourself when you've learned how to say no. They are the Martyrs and the Not-Worthy Women.

Who are the Martyrs? They are the women who:

>> do everything for everybody,

>> are driven by guilt,

>> expect you to be just like them, and

>> cancel their own plans so they can attend everything they are invited to.

When the Martyrs say "it must be nice," it's coming from a place of resentment and frustration. Why can you take time for yourself while they are running around pleasing everyone? Who allowed you to do that?

I have learned and grown so much from these women. It only takes a few mental hits from these women to feel the pain. It is a pain that robs you of internal joy and that carries a very subtle undertone of guilt. They give you only minutes to defend yourself before they walk away, most likely to gossip about you with another Martyr.

I have watched Martyrs and studied them in the midst of gatherings, so I know how they work. They arrive early, they give up their free time to help, and they lack substance because they spend very little time nourishing themselves. They are focused on how they can be the "savior" for someone else. They live in a state of denial, not spending time on what makes them happy, because they are too busy trying to please others. They stay late to help clean up, even though their kids are screaming because they just want to go home. These Martyrs are clever women. They stay to clean up, noticing who has left the party and keeping a mental note of it to throw it back in your face at a later date. They are slick, all right.

A friend once told me her husband's family was full of Martyrs. She suffered for years, defending herself, trying to make up clever, believable excuses as to why she couldn't attend certain gatherings. One sister-in-law actually gave her a list of all the parties she was "expected" to attend in the upcoming months. My friend, so angry and now in her power, smiled and took the list. And didn't show up for a single one of the parties. Here is what the Martyr sister-in-law said to the Martyr mother-in-law, "I don't know why she isn't here, I gave her that list two months ago."

My friend had finally begun to understand how these women work and she didn't want to be part of it. It did cause some major tension within her husband's family, but she had no choice but to distance herself from them. We all supported her through tears of sadness and anger, we problem-solved and even role-played what she would say and how to say it. She is a much happier person without the constant mind games of difficult women. Having supportive friends was a major factor in my friend's struggle for survival. We spent hours giving her strength and reminding her she was not the problem. We also reinforced for her that this was not the right way to be treated by anyone, let alone family.

You also run across these women at your child's school. They volunteer for everything, put in long hours and get annoyed when others don't follow suit. You can hear them venting their frustrations about the lack of help all the way out the door.

I confess that the last thing I want to be doing on my time off in my busy life is to help set up tables for a craft fair. I just can't do it. I will buy treats for the treat table, but time is not something I want to give right now. My point: people give in different ways. Some have the money, some have the time and some are stretched to the max and can't give anything at the moment. The Martyrs want to judge others, but it's healthier to say "I'll do what I can when I can and not everyone will do exactly the same as I do."

The other woman you may hear "it must be nice" or "how could you say no?" from is the Not-Worthy Woman. You can recognize **the Not-Worthy Women** because they:

>> have low self esteem,

>> feel not worthy of taking enjoyable time for themselves, and

>> believe they are not deserving of good things.

When they say "it must be nice," it's coming from a sad, worn-out place. I always encourage these women to believe they deserve and are worthy of time to renew their spirit and nourish their soul.

The Not-Worthy Women I've met have had low self-esteem since they were young. For whatever reason, they never were able to gain a sense of worth and self-esteem. Unlike the feeling of pure annoyance I get when I meet Martyrs, I feel a great sense of sadness when I meet the Not-Worthy Women. I watch how they walk and interact with people, their heads down and their posture introverted. I do my best to offer words of encouragement, but it often falls on deaf ears. They believe or are being told at home that they don't deserve the happiness that comes from setting boundaries, saying no and taking time off from daily chores. They live in the grind day after day, surrounding themselves with other women who are guilt-ridden and who have little pleasure. And by pleasure, I mean leaving the kids with a sitter or your husband so you can grab a coffee. I'm not even talking about leaving for three weeks on an Alaskan cruise by yourself (as good as that sounds).

The Not-Worthy Women can guilt you in a different way; they can make you question if you too are Not-Worthy. If you hang out with them long enough, their guilt and sadness can stick to you. Before long, you might also have your head hung low, not feeling deserving of all the good things life has to offer. Be aware of the company you keep. Some women I speak to in my coaching sessions have said they get guilt placed on them from so many different directions it makes their head spin (and ache!). They didn't know what hit them until they had time to process the not-so-good feelings they were experiencing. Take note of your feelings and spend as little time as possible with women who do not uplift you or support you.

4. Sidestep the Joy Suckers

Warning: Avoid negative people who will suck the joy right out of you. Here's how to recognize the Joy Suckers:

>> You will feel depleted and annoyed after spending time with them.

>> They are negative and go out of their way to make you feel negative and miserable, too.

You know these people… the Negative Nellies who walk around with a dark cloud over them. I am not talking about people who are going through a tough time. We all have our ups and downs in life, some folks just stay down. The Joy Suckers demonstrate constant negativity.

Does this sound familiar? You are excited about something, happy and glowing. Because the Joy Sucker sees life through misery-colored glasses (as opposed to rose-colored ones), they can't wait to tell you how and why it won't work out for you, why you shouldn't do this or that, and try to instill fear in you. Do you know any Joy Suckers?

When I ask others why they still hang out with the Joy Suckers, (and/or Martyrs or Not-Worthy Women), they often say "I feel bad for them" or "her kid plays with my kid so I am stuck listening to her."

Be careful with this type of thinking. Choose wisely the company you keep. And choose you should! You have the power to choose, so embrace that power.

When we set boundaries and take time for ourselves, we feel happy and content! Surround yourself with people who are like the person you want to be.

When we are in the company of inspiring people, we in turn become inspired. You want to be like your positive role models, you want to glow with confidence and positivity. I believe you can be that person! Confidence is contagious.

Does your social network contain negative people who always grumble and complain or want advice about change but never take it? You know the type—they really seem like they want to change yet never can get out of their own way to do it. They make excuses about why they can't take even small steps. If you are hanging around with friends like these, find new friends! Or at the very least, spend less time with Joy Suckers.

As you can imagine, I don't spend much of my free time with unhealthy women. My support group is full of strong, confident women who have direction and a strong sense of self-worth. I am cordial to Martyr Women, Not-Worthy Women and Joy Suckers, but I don't spend much time with them. Do you? Are your friends Martyrs or Not-Worthy or Joy Suckers… or are you one of them?

journal entry

Be True to Yourself

Can you disappoint another to be true to yourself?

Can you say no to someone else even if you know they will be upset with you?

Do you give in and go places you don't want to be to avoid the conflict it may cause if you say no?

If you believe in your heart that no is the correct answer, don't hesitate to say it. Be true to yourself always.

Do you know Martyr Women?

If yes, how do they make you feel?

Be True to Yourself (continued)

Do you know Not-Worthy Women?

_____

_____

Are you "not worthy" or have you felt that way in the past?

_____

_____

_____

What helped you get to a more confident, worthy place?

_____

_____

_____

_____

_____

Do you surround yourself with any Joy Suckers? Do you feel annoyed and frustrated when you leave them? How can you stay away from them?

_____

_____

_____

_____

_____

_____

> *"When you are desperate for time to yourself and you feel way out of balance in your life, it's time to start saying NO."*
>
> –JULIE McGRATH

Why I Say NO

What I came to realize is that if you choose not to go to a wedding or a party, everyone else will still have a great time. The world doesn't stop if you decide not to go, even if you are told differently. There are always a few events we "have to" attend, even though we don't always want to. I understand that and comply when I must. However, it is so empowering to feel able to choose what events you want to attend.

Never allow yourself to be made to feel guilty about not attending an event or saying no to a request. My perspective is that if you don't want to come to my event full of love and joy for me, then I don't want you there. How many times have you gone somewhere and ended up staring out the window wishing you were someplace else? I wait all year for summer, as the New England climate only grants us three months (if we are lucky) of hot, sunny days. I love those days and soak up every minute. After a long, cold winter, I feel re-energized when the days are hot. If you invite me to a bridal shower or baby shower or some other event on a sunny summer weekend afternoon, my most likely reply is "no, thank you." I won't give up my limited sunny, warm days! Does that sound selfish to you? I hope not. I would be annoyed and frustrated if I had to spend my summer weekends running from party to party. Everyone at the event will still have a fantastic time even though I am not there. I am sure of it.

Be honest with yourself. What do you need to do to feel good inside? Not the superficial stuff like retail therapy, getting a facial, a manicure—all great—but what is it that makes you glow from the inside out? There are things you used to do that maybe do not stimulate you any longer, friendships you might have outgrown, relationships that have run their course and jobs that need to be changed. Think about the more difficult stuff, the stuff that makes you cry, reflect and cry some more.

5. Keep It Real.

 The fifth and final weapon you need so you can defend against losing yourself to family is simple: keep it real.

I laugh when I read posts like this on Facebook: "Happy anniversary to my best friend! I married him 20 years ago and he is my best friend and the best father to our children." Why do I laugh? I laugh because earlier that day, the same woman was complaining about her spouse's dedication to his job, how she never sees him and how the children prefer to be with their grandparents rather than their own father. This has been a constant complaint of hers throughout the six years I have known her. So why put on a happy face and pretend? I simply can't do that. When she wrote that, she was really thinking "Happy Anniversary, you're pathetic! I can't believe I made it this far without leaving you or putting a pillow over your face when you are sleeping. You are an awful father and I am heartbroken I married you, wake up and pay attention to me, you jerk!"

If you and your husband are having difficulties, when it is your anniversary you don't feel like you married your best friend; in fact, it may feel more like you married your enemy. Despite the social pressures we all feel (and the tendency for people to "spin" things on social media like Facebook), you don't need to glamorize your marriage. Instead, just say it like it is, "It's been better," or don't say anything at all.

Posting on Facebook and telling people our lives are fine gives us that hope that maybe they will be. Maybe we can convince ourselves we are happy. Just like those women who never slow down. They run from place to place, all weekend long, all week long, never stopping to reflect. Why? For most, it is simply too painful. If you stay busy you never have time to think about what is not right, so you never have to deal with it! Brilliant! What is your happiness rating on a scale of 1 to 10? I mean *real* happiness, not just what your Facebook friends will see. Are you really at 3 or 4 instead of the happier 9 or 10?

I know in my own life, there are times when people ask me about my daughter and I just want to reply, "she's a devious stubborn little witch and she's kicking my ass."

There are plenty of other times where I'm likely to describe her as a sweet, beautiful, funny and full-of-big-kisses girl. Our perspective on our lives shifts from moment to moment—be honest about what you are feeling when you feel it.

Be honest with yourself about what is happening in your world. Surround yourself with people who allow you to be real and don't dismiss how you feel. Remember how at the beginning of the book I told you the most freeing moment was when my friend told me, "you don't have to like your kids all the time"? What if she had said the opposite to me? Something to the effect of, "maybe you are not doing it right? Maybe you should see a therapist or something, why are you so upset?" I was in a vulnerable spot and her response could have made me feel even worse about myself.

We all have different experiences of motherhood (and fatherhood, for that matter). What one person finds enjoyable might not be for the other. I was at a work meeting and a man commented that his two little boys were up all night and it was killing him; he was exhausted and looked worn down. Here are the two responses he got:

Me: I am so sorry, I have been there, it sucks but you will get through it. It will pass, hang in there.

My co-worker: I loved that stage, I would wake up and hold them. It was one of my favorite times with them, I enjoyed it.

Now which comment do you think made him feel worse? Oh, c'mon, you enjoyed being up every night? Great, keep it to yourself. This poor guy is losing it! Insinuating that he should not only like it, but enjoy it is not making him feel any better.

I fully understand that if you have only one child and he/she is easy and good-natured, there are many stories in this book you will not relate to. One difficult, stubborn child can throw even the strongest mom over the edge. Be grateful yours is easy, but please, never judge those of us who are up every night with a non-sleeper, non-napper and big pooper. It can be rough.

I remember when I turned into Psycho Mom one night. I was tired and frustrated with my children's behavior. They share a room, so when they get all charged up, it's hell putting them to bed. After maybe 10 trips upstairs to get them to settle down,

I lost it. I flung open the door, almost pulling it off the hinges, crying and yelling, and threw all their toys into the closet, breaking some of them. The kids were crying and when my husband came home, they said to him in a whisper, "I think Mommy broke all our toys."

I felt horrible. I hate expelling such negative energy and I hate when I can't keep it together. The next morning I went to my 6 a.m. boot camp with red, swollen eyes from crying. I sat with my circle of women and shared what had occurred the night before, with my head hung low and fresh tears in my eyes. Without hesitation, each woman chuckled, hugged me and shared her own story of "Psycho Mom" behavior.

"I once cleared off the top of my son's dresser right into a trash bag, one clean sweep."

"I opened the window and threw the toys right out."

"My daughter whined and cried that my son had more Oreo cookies than she did and I lost it. I grabbed all the cookies and stepped on them I was so furious."

We all have those moments. These are real moments. No one is getting physically hurt, but all good mommies lose it at times. As long as you have the self-control to calm yourself *before* anyone gets hurt, don't feel so bad. My kids have never brought up that night and I apologized for my behavior the following day when I could think clearly. If you find that you are losing your temper more often and becoming abusive in your language to your children, please talk to someone you trust about it. It is normal to get upset, but getting carried away is not allowed. Seek help through your pediatrician or therapist, and call your local parent hotline or crisis team if you need immediate assistance.

Do you see why it is so important for us to take care of ourselves emotionally? We would have way more "psycho mom" occurrences if we never got a break from our children, if we never had a chance to take care of ourselves and put back all that we give out. When you are in the company of women who don't judge you, who share with you, it makes all the difference. Let those superficial friends exit your social circle.

It's all in the company you keep. When you think about your social support circle, do you feel the feelings below?

>> I feel good being with you.

>> I like how I feel in your presence.

>> Just sitting beside you nourishes me.

>> Knowing you are in the next room provides me comfort and security.

>> Even when you are not physically with me, I feel your presence around me and I smile.

>> When I close my eyes, I still see you and I feel fulfilled.

>> When I am hurting, I see the hurt in your eyes too, you feel my pain and move toward me to soothe it.

>> I am content knowing you are happy.

>> Long after we part, I reflect on our conversation and I feel myself growing in a positive way.

>> Laughing with you gives me such joy. It is a joy from within and touches my heart.

>> Your hug uplifts my spirit.

>> With you by my side, I know I am capable of achieving all my dreams.

Surround yourself with friends, family and companions who engulf you with their love and bring out the best in you. Seek to be fulfilled. All things are possible when we have the right people beside us.

When you set clear boundaries, you gain more time for yourself and more time for JOY. I encourage you to be honest about the status of your joy cup. Does it feel half-full or half-empty? **If your joy cup is only one-quarter full, and the rest is obligations, negative friends and exhausting children, you have some work to do**. Start where you are to change it. Don't be embarrassed or ashamed, be real about how you feel. That is the starting point for a life of joy. Realize what is happening in your world, what is not joyful and doesn't add to your happiness, and then decide to change it. Moving at the speed of light day after day will allow you to bypass how you are really feeling, covering it up with constant noise and movement. Your happiness will be postponed until you can sit in silence long enough to ask yourself, "Am I really happy?" If you have always had strong friends around you and even stronger boundaries, lead the way.

In workshops, women often ask me what their next move in life might be. I only wish I had the skill to predict that for them! This is not what you want to hear, but it is the truth. You already know where you need to be and what feels like the right direction. It's that inner voice guiding you, supporting you and telling you right from wrong. Yes, I am quite sure you have that voice; are you paying enough attention to hear it? Be still and keep reading, let's find out together.

CHAPTER 7

Listen to Your Inner Voice and Re-ignite Your Passion

Stay engaged in your life; a constant love affair with your life will keep you beaming with joy and fulfillment.

....

Years go by full of diaper-changing, sleepless nights, play dates and PTO meetings, and at some point, each one of us looks in the mirror and asks, "What the hell happened to *me*?"

That woman looking back at you is not the person you once were—a vibrant, confident, alive person. Now you see an exhausted version of yourself that feels soft, less confident and barely smiles. This chapter is about resurrecting the strong, confident woman you once were and still are… she's just gotten a little lost in the motherhood process.

When I do my Joy Course, (a five-week joy group for women) I am often surprised at how many women give up what brings them joy in their lives. When I ask the ladies to write about what they do for fun or what brings them fulfillment, *besides their family*, most look down and fumble with their pen.

For most women, the change is not abrupt. Most women don't say, "Well, now that I am a mother, I am not going out with my friends or going to the gym again or doing the things I love to do." After hearing countless stories, I have realized that it's a very subtle process, this loss of self, one that takes place over months and years. It happens as we slowly give in to the daily grind and give up on what takes effort and energy in our lives—even if these are the very things that make us feel complete and whole as a person.

For some of us, self-care is such a priority that we don't hesitate to keep those activities in our lives. It helps when you are part of a club or a team that counts on you to show up and encourages you to make that time. Women involved this way tend to keep it alive and actually don't think twice about the time it takes away from their home lives. My friend Eve is an inspiration to me.

Eve was part of a running club long before marriage and children. When she met her husband in the running club, there was no need to explain or fight for the time to run. They each took turns with their running schedules and which race they would run. When their children came, they could no longer train for races together, but that didn't seem to bother them, as long as they could continue with the camaraderie of friendships of the running club. This fulfilled Eve in an important way, because she loved to run and she loved her friends at the club; seeing them weekly kept enthusiasm and joy in her life. Her babies were born and she didn't skip a beat in her world. She remained true to her passions and felt like herself in all ways.

When you decide to let what you love take a back seat, putting it back into your life after a long absence is often difficult to do. Taking short breaks here and there due to your schedule or your children's schedules is normal, just make sure you have a goal—written down on paper—that states when you commit to engaging again. Once you fill up that time with other stuff, errands and housework, it is hard to find that hour again.

My best advice… DON'T GIVE IT UP in the first place.

Let me repeat this just one more time, a little louder: **DON'T GIVE IT UP in the first place!**

But what if you already did give it up? Here's how to get it back. First, try your best to negotiate "time off," hire babysitters, and put yourself and your time on the high-priority list. Don't be afraid to share with your husband what satisfies you and what your needs are. These needs of yours are just as important as (if not more important than) the needs of anyone else in the family. Remember, you cannot give what you don't have. If you are not happy, excited and in love with your life, how do you give that to those you love?

For many of us, time goes by so fast we feel like we never saw it coming. We thought not taking care of ourselves goes with being a mother; that coming in last is what Mommy gets when children enter the mix. I hear so often from women who give up what they want, "Oh I am just sacrificing, that's what we mothers do."

Yes, they're right—sort of. For those of us who give birth, it is a sacrifice to give up our bodies, and to make so many daily sacrifices of time, but why should our dreams, our wants, our sense of self be sacrificed as well? What good does it do our children when we put ourselves at the bottom of the list? When we stop living *our* lives and begin just living for our children?

Stop for a moment, and quiet your mind long enough to figure out your hopes and dreams. What would make you happy, content and joyful? What is your wish right here, today? What is one wish, goal or dream you have?

Think about it…

"What do I want out of life?"

When you respond, I encourage you to be specific. So many of us answer in general terms, "I want to be happy" or "I want to feel good." Who doesn't?

The key lies in the "how." How can you make that happen? What makes you happy?

For some of us, it is "I want to feel _____ in my life, but have no idea how."

So what can you do to get there? What do you need to do to put yourself in a state of "feeling good"? What effort must you make, what work must you do to be happy? If the "how" wasn't part of your original answer, go back and finish it here…

I want [SOMETHING SPECIFIC] _____

and [DOING SOMETHING SPECIFIC] _____

will make that happen.

When I ask women what they want out of life that has nothing to do with being a mother, I usually get an answer connected to their spouses, children or family. It's wonderful to be connected to your family. It is refreshing to have quality family time. But what might you want for *you*? You as a woman who has dreams, goals and interests that do not involve or revolve around the family unit? If your answer is "I don't know," that is okay. I wrote this book and you're reading it for that very reason, to help you figure it out and reclaim the joy in your life as a confident woman.

Does this person sound like you?

Did you once have a clear vision of what you wanted in your life, but then a busy life took over and hasn't stopped, not giving you a chance to think about it? Did you let go of it years ago? Or did you ever really know?

Losing sight of ourselves happens to the best of us and it's not necessarily limited to women who have become mothers. There's good news: it's reversible. However, it takes effort to get there. This chapter will get the ball rolling for you, giving you a much-needed push (or for some of you, a gentle reminder) to remember what you want.

Let's walk through some exercises and put some thought into what YOU want. Not what others want for you. Not what your family thinks will make you happy nor what your partner believes will satisfy you. I am talking about what *you* want on the inside that makes you glow, that ignites a fire within your soul to say... **This is what I want and here is how I am going to get it.**

I'm going to ask you to consider tough questions about your wants, needs, true happiness and satisfaction, and encourage you to put a plan in place to make them happen. Why? Because you are worthy and deserve it! (But more on the worthy part in the next chapter.)

Let's start by determining what you want in your life... let's talk about passion.

Passion: What's Yours?

>> What ignites a glow in you?

>> What invigorates you?

>> What lights a fire in your soul?

Passion! I love that word! Think about those questions above. Can you easily answer them? Are the answers on the tip of your tongue because you have worked on keeping a passionate life?

What ignites a glow in you?

You know when you are glowing. How does it feel? OH, SO GOOD! Has it been some time since you felt ignited by passion? Passion fuels us, drives us and gives us a reason to get up in the morning. The sparks from the fire fuel the drive and motivation. When I speak about passion, most people think I am talking about sex. They equate passion and sex. I will get to the sex in a minute, but for now I am talking about passion as it relates to your everyday life. When you're passionate about your hobbies, interests or accomplishments, you glow. When you glow, people take notice. You don't have to be a beauty queen to be noticed. You just need to glow from the inside out.

If you've ever spent much time in nightclubs, chances are you understand how your inner glow often takes second place to your outer appearance. In real life, you have much more to offer than being aesthetically pleasing. People do take notice when you are radiating a glow from within. Read on for a man's perspective on a woman's inner glow and how important it is.

"I first noticed Kara when we were working out at the same gym. We took the same exercise class. She would walk into this room full of people just coming from work, tired, cranky and wearing their day on their shoulders, but not Kara. She always had friends surrounding her, gabbing and laughing, and she glowed. I could tell she was a quality woman, not conventionally gorgeous with the perfect body like the other girls, but gorgeous to me. I had to be near her and know her. I slowly made my way to her, trying as best I could to infiltrate her social circle and not be seen as a pervert. At each class, I watched her come into the room; she never knew she commanded such attention. She had assumed all the eyes were going to the hot young girls in tight spandex. True, all the guys noticed them. That is a fleeting feeling, very different from noticing and admiring the way Kara carried herself. Kara was confident and real. Her inner glow is what i love so much. End of story, I asked her out, she said yes, and now she is my wife."

What invigorates you?

People take notice when you are radiating a light from within. You give off a glow that shows people you are living on purpose. People gravitate to you. They want to know what you are doing, why you are feeling so fulfilled and when and where they can get some. **Passion is like an adrenaline rush.** It consumes our being, offers a fresh perspective on life and fills us with joy.

Feed your passion. Grow with excitement—remember how it felt to be elated, to be consumed with excitement? If you can't remember, it may be time to sit in silent reflection, clear the chatter in your head, and re-discover what once inspired you. Seek the sparks, my friend. The excitement and joy awaits you. Here's an example from my client Gina, in her own words:

"I enjoyed my college years because I was so politically active. We had a great Democratic Party group and we would do fundraisers for local candidates and spend hours holding signs at election time. I actually got an article published about women and politics. I was passionate about certain issues and I sought out candidates who held the same beliefs. Fast-forward 10 years, I'm a mother with three children and a husband. My husband was injured in a work accident and that has left me little time for myself. Talk about waking up one day thinking, 'Am I really this woman looking back at me in the bathroom mirror?'

"Ugh! I was disgusted. I needed my hair cut, I had gained 30 pounds, I had acne breakouts from stress, but what struck me most was that I had no passion in my eyes. I was depleted and living on automatic pilot. After months of trying my best to get back into shape and prioritizing my life, I realized I hadn't been involved in an election of any type in seven years. There were years I couldn't even turn the TV on to watch the candidates for fear I would be too stirred up and could do nothing about it. I was ready now. Wishing I never gave it up but not living in regret, I got involved again. Within hours of plotting my moves, deciding which cause and candidate to endorse, I could feel the excitement flow back into my body. It was like no other feeling. I felt alive again."

journal entry

Passion

How would you describe passion? What word/words come to mind?

_____

_____

_____

Look at the description you just wrote. Have you ever felt that way?

_____

Are you leading a passionate life now?

_____

Are you passionate about a cause or a movement?

_____

journal entry

Passion (continued)

Or do you feel like you are leading a mundane, ordinary, non-exciting existence?

Has it been a while since you felt ignited?

Are you stuck?

Do you need a passion renewal?

Were you once leading a passionate life? Reflect back to that time for a moment. What was it like? What were you doing? How did you feel?

What stirs your passion? Renews your spirit? Makes you feel good? Make a list below.

Look at your list. Which activities do you wish you could do more often? Have you already integrated some into your daily or weekly routine?

What lights a fire in your soul?

We deserve to live passionate lives, lives that are colorful and juicy. You are worthy and you deserve it. In his book *Flow*, author Mihaly Csikszentmihalyi explains that flow refers to "joy, creativity, the process of total involvement with life." After doing years of research on what makes people happy, he concluded, "People were happiest when they were just talking to one another. When they gardened, knitted, or were involved in a hobby; all of these activities require few material resources, but they demand a relatively high investment of psychic energy. Leisure that uses up external resources (power boating, driving, watching TV), however, often requires less attention, and as a consequence it generally provides less memorable rewards."

Flow moments are amazing, exciting and refreshing. We need more such moments in our lives because they feed our souls and genuinely bring a joy to us that lasts long after the associated activity has stopped. Seek them daily, not just once a year when you go on a girl's weekend or a family vacation. Seek them in your life often. For each one of us they will be different. The things that give me flow moments will be different than those that bring you "flow."

I can tell you what doesn't bring on flow moments—housework! Don't spend all your time making your house look immaculate. If you hang out with people who judge you on how clean your home is, you are hanging out with the wrong people. Devoting too much time to chores will make for a not-so-happy lady. Children can have many chores, and chores they should do! Can you leave the laundry on the stairs so you can squeeze in 30 minutes on the treadmill? Can you walk by the dishes in the sink so you can catch that spin class at the gym? Can you wash the towels tomorrow so you can finish painting your masterpiece today? Can you organize the junk drawer later so you can finish writing in your journal? Get my point, ladies? Many things can wait, and non-important chores can wait so you can have a few fulfilling moments before the really important stuff comes calling, i.e. your children.

Focus on the experiences in life, not all the stuff. We are so good at buying tons of stuff. Electronics, clothing, home décor, toys upon toys for our kids. How much is enough? Does the happiness last after your new car is a year old? Think about experiences you had as a child or that you've had with your children. You may or may not take pictures, but you can always share memories and reminisce. For a lifetime!!

I grew up in a simple, small home. The basement could have been turned into another playroom, but it wasn't high on my parents' to-do list. In fact, it wasn't until they were selling their home did they actually get it fixed up. Instead of spending money on that when we already had a nice living room, they preferred to spend the money on fun evenings going out to dinner and taking exciting vacations. That happened two years in a row, each one better than the next. We went as a family to Club Med, and believe me, a Club Med vacation was amazing to a fifteen-year-old, and created memories for a lifetime. In fact, I just reconnected with a guy I met there over 25 years ago, and we both laughed at the good times we had at Club Med! These experiences don't necessarily have to be wild adventures. They can be quiet moments with friends or a loud, hilarious adult game night. When was the last time you bought some fun board games and invited friends over to play? Try it, I guarantee many laughs! Kids aren't the only ones who can enjoy board games!

journal entry

Are You in the Flow?

What are your "flow" moments?

_____

_____

_____

_____

_____

journal entry

How often do feel you are doing exactly what you want to be doing?
_____

_____

How often do you jump up and down with excitement and shout out YES!
_____

_____

How often do you wake up with a smile eager to start your day?
☐ Never   ☐ Seldom   ☐ Often   ☐ Very Often   ☐ Every Day

>> If you answered "often," "very often" or "every day," then you are in good
JOY shape. Congratulations on a flow-filled life!

>> If you answered "never" or "seldom," don't endure one more "blah" mo-
ment of your existence. Start re-filling your joy cup now! I am thrilled you
are reading this book and hope you can start your journey to joy, passion
and excitement right away.

Is Sexual Passion Part of Your Joy?

Were you the one who yelled out "SEX!" when I asked what brings you passion in your
life? Well, good for you! Glad you are enjoying what is natural and ready for you at
any time. So, let's talk about sex. Won't you join me? Keep reading.

Sex and passion, that's a fantastic combination. Do you have it in your life right now?
Let's get honest... How can you feel passionate and ready for a night of lovemaking
when you are not taking care of yourself? If you are sixty pounds overweight and
don't feel great about your body, you may not want to be touched and rubbed with
that massage oil sitting neglected in your beauty supply bucket. Or maybe you're
annoyed with your husband because he didn't do the dishes again. How can you

fully enjoy a night of pleasure when you are so tired from being with your children non-stop that all you can think is, "No way I'm having sex. What if we accidentally create another one of these monsters?"

So you tell your partner again, "Not tonight, honey."

What do I say to that?

ARE YOU CRAZY?

Sex is amazing. Sex is fantastic. It is a time for closeness. A time to have the heat turned up between two people. A time to dress up in those gorgeous black boots and watch how your husband's eyes light up.

Yes, ladies, we are busy women. We do so much for everyone and try to cram as much as we can into every waking moment. Sometimes we don't like our children, our husbands, our lives. It's all exhausting. But at the end of the day (or the beginning), we should definitely be getting a good, strong, earth-shattering orgasm. One that curls our toes until we get a foot cramp. Don't we deserve that? Yes, we do, but I know what you are thinking... who has the time and who feels sexy?

First of all, I say make the time. Sex feels good. Hell, sex feels great! Or it should. If you are not having an orgasm, why should you do it otherwise? I want you to enjoy sex.

If you are married with small children, you definitely need that release of hot energy flowing through you. Don't wait for the house to be quiet and for the children to be at a sleepover. Don't wait for all the romance you had when you were dating... the candles, oils and lotions... or the foreplay and sweet words. Don't get me wrong, I still want you to have all that, but the reality is, a quick spark is just as good.

All you need is five minutes. Kids are outside playing? Daddy and Mommy need to change the light bulb, be back in five minutes. Or put the television on, throw random snacks in front of the kids, run upstairs, lock the door and romp. Sometimes you might not even make it to the bed. Perfect. Let me repeat, all you need is five minutes. "My kids know not to come to our room on weekend mornings until we open our door," says Jennifer, a 36-year-old working mother of two small girls. "My husband and I are just as hot now as we were twelve years ago, now we just realize we have less intimate time and have to get down to business quickly."

If you find that it takes you longer, try something new. Grab a vibrator and the release will be quick and intense. According to Goddess Michelle from Athena's Adult Toys and Novelties, "Most women require foreplay to arrive at an orgasm during sex. A good vibrator can offer direct stimulation to just the right spot at just the right speed when you don't have time to enjoy the journey!"

Now for the "feeling sexy" part... I know you're tired. Worn out. Stressed. It's true, who wants to get naked when we have been dealing with whiny kids and a messy house all day long? My advice? Hire a housecleaner. Put your kids in daycare for half the day to get back some sanity. Take care of your body. Exercise. If you are overweight and unhappy with your body, move into action. Do something about it. You owe it to yourself to feel good in every way. Tell your hubby he will get IT more if he helps OUT more. Does he really need to be told this? Yup. So tell him.

I challenge you to embrace your sexuality. Don't let time slip away not indulging in your sexuality. Let it loosen you up and break the confines of your daily life. Let the passion lift you into the extraordinary. Even for just five minutes.

I met Manda at a women's retreat a few years ago. She acknowledged there have been ups and downs through the course of her 20-year relationship, but one thing that has consistently gotten better is the sex. She told me, "We know each other's bodies and once in a while he will even come up with a new move that takes me to another world. Sex for us is fun, playful and creative. It is our private world and it is a slice of heaven, even just for 10 minutes. I do my best to leave what transpired that day out of the bedroom. My children have never been allowed to sleep in my bed. If they are sick or have nightmares, we sleep in their bed. This is the only sacred space allowed for just my husband and me. I am a sexual being as much as he is and I want to enjoy it all while I can! He loves massaging my body with oil and I love receiving it! Once in a while we watch porn, use toys, I dress up with sexy nighties and high heels and after that orgasm, I am in a different, much happier state of mind! Too much of a good thing is WONDERFUL!"

"True passion is intoxicating and invigorating, soothing and sensuous, magical and mystical. I just thought you should know what you're in for."
–SARAH BAN BREATHNACH, *SOMETHING MORE: EXCAVATING YOUR AUTHENTIC SELF*

Don't settle for boring. Don't settle for bland. Brighten yourself up. Live your passion. You are responsible for your own joy. Yes, you! Create it for yourself! Don't depend on others to make you happy or more passionate. You hold all the keys in your hand, my friend, for unlocking the passion, self-discovery, joy and happiness. When you begin to listen to your inner voice, you will find your joyful path isn't so far off. It has been there all along, waiting for you to follow it. When you focus less on material goods and more on healthy experiences, you will feel more satisfied, more content.

Once you are at that fulfilled place, how do you stay there? How do you sustain that most wonderful feeling of invigoration and passion? Do you feel worthy of overflowing with joy? Will you deflect it to someone else who you believe is more worthy than you? In the next chapter, we dive head-first into the loaded topic of worth.

CHAPTER 8

Worthy and Wanting the Good Life: Reclaim Yourself as a Strong, Confident Woman

"How wrong it is for a woman to expect the man to build the world she wants, rather than to create it herself."
—ANAÏS NIN

Now you know *what* you want in your life… it's time to figure out how to get it. Ideally, this is an easy step, right? If you want to go back to school and get an advanced degree, for example, why not just enroll in an online university or local college and start classes? Simple, right?

Wouldn't it be amazing if it *were* that simple?

For a few of you, it is. You will register and buy your books, never pausing a moment as you work to make your dreams a reality. But most likely, if you are one of those women, you aren't reading this book (or at least you are just skimming this chapter). Most likely, you are staring at your response to the questions in the previous chapter about what you want in life and saying to yourself…

I can't do that.

Or, *no way, I shouldn't do that.*

Or, *that's crazy.*

Or some version of the above. Instead of jumping feet-first into pursuing your desire, you are coming up with some excuse for why you can't or shouldn't.

There is a reason you aren't living the life you truly dream of. Something is getting in the way of you pursuing your goals. Don't worry, many women get stuck at this point and don't take the next step.

Why? What stops us?

While you may offer various reasons why you won't go back to school (lack of money and/or time, no local schools), these are the socially acceptable "excuses." These are external challenges you must find a solution to, but they are not what is actually stopping you.

The real obstacles to overcome are the ones inside of you.

Feeling worthy of pursuing your dreams or even having a fantastic day is the most essential and crucial component of leading a joyful and fulfilling life. You have to feel worthy of receiving what you want! If you want the good stuff to happen in your life, do you deflect it out of guilt or feelings that you are unworthy to feel such amazing joy? Sadly, many women think they shouldn't be super-happy. They can rationalize feeling okay, but feeling utter bliss might be too indulgent. I encourage you to seek that blissful feeling, feel worthy of allowing all of the good, happy emotions to flood your being. Yes, you are worthy. You were *never* not worthy.

I laugh when people say, "I am so happy now that I am waiting for something bad to happen." How sad is that? You deserve the feeling of joy, you don't need to counter it with something bad to knock you off your high. It doesn't work that way, unless you believe it does and you want to be knocked off the high. If you believe you are only worthy of a certain amount of happiness, then that is all you will experience. Want that joy for yourself and for everyone in your life. They are worthy, too.

NEWSFLASH: If you are surrounding yourself with people who treat you as though you are not worthy of an exciting life, you are hanging out with the wrong crowd! Believe you are ready right now, right this instant, to be overwhelmed with joy.

Consider how you might have started feeling unworthy, a process that happens over time. Here is one way it can start. Suppose you are planning two fun getaway weekends in two months, and you are excited and ready. You tell your friends and they make comments like:

"Didn't you just go away? Why are you going away again so soon?"

"Must be nice, I wish I could go away two months in a row."

"You are leaving your kids for two weekends? Wow, I wouldn't do that if I were you."

Little comments like these can start the unworthy cycle moving. Most of the time you don't even realize it. The comments come at you, you internalize them and they become a part of your inner thoughts about yourself and your happiness—but only if you let them! SO DON'T!

These are the comments I want you to hear:

"Good for you! You deserve that time away!"

"You work so hard, you need that break."

"I want to come next year! So happy for you!"

Yes, these are the comments of true friends who want to see you happy and who believe, just as you need to, that you are worthy of living the good life. Open your arms and your heart and let all the joy flow right into you! Now is your time!

As women, each of us has a mile-long mental or handwritten list of all the activities we need to get done for the day or week (or lifetime… yes, I'm not ashamed to say "change the lightbulb in the hallway" has been on my list for years).

Right now, what are the top five items on your list that you have to handle today? What about for the week?

Write them down if you don't already have a list on the refrigerator or in your smartphone.

1. _____

2. _____

3. _____

4. _____

5. _____

Look at that list again… where are YOU on your important TO DO list?

If you listed 10 items, are you even on the list?

I bet everyone around you is on that list—the kids, spouse, neighbor, mail carrier… but not you. Somehow over the years, you got pushed to the back. Your goals and dreams are on the back burner because you have too many "I SHOULD INSTEADs" in your life.

>> I **should** really use my free time to do laundry… **instead** of going for a nice walk to reconnect with nature.

>> I **should** go to that bridal shower for my sister's friend I met once last year… **instead** of going to see that movie I've been dying to see.

>> I **should** do this for that person… **instead** of taking the day off to go out and play while everyone else is at work or school.

>> I **should** take these few minutes before picking up my kids at school to balance my checkbook… **instead** of sitting quietly so I can hear my own thoughts in my head about what I want for myself, not what everyone else wants from me.

Most of us women, with or without children, possess that built-in nurturing nature … that feeling like we want to make **everyone** around us content and happy. And if everyone around us is happy, then we are happy, and only then, if there is a little piece of time or any tiny bit of energy left at the end of the day, then maybe, JUST MAYBE, we can grab some happiness. Do something we want to do.

And then it starts to creep into our being. Maybe? Possibly? For me? Can I? Can I leave the laundry on the stairs, can I leave the sink full of dishes, can I not make the bed today, can I leave out just one thing on my to do list so I creep closer to the top five? Can I? If I am not too depleted or too tired, maybe I can be joyful in a hobby?

Yeah, right! I am too tired and I make excuses, so I watch mindless television, get into bed and do it all over again the next day. Maybe joy just isn't for me.

Sound familiar?

Maybe you've heard that phrase… "If mama ain't happy, ain't nobody happy."

It's true. Or it should be… so put *that* "should" on your list.

It is easier to give in to the grind of the everyday routine. If you just keep that fast pace, never slow down, you will never realize what you are missing. If you are living in isolation and moving at a very slow pace, start believing you are worthy of new experiences. Start saying yes to joy, putting more activities into your daily life that bring you fulfillment. You never know how truly joyful you can be and how your heart and soul can rejoice when you are fulfilling yourself on a deep level.

It doesn't have to be an expensive vacation or a life-changing event. I am just talking about going out to dinner with your girlfriends and laughing. Or going to the beach to watch the waves for an hour, to soothe and relax you. It is these simple, easy, joyful moments that you are worthy of participating in and taking advantage of. We need to put ourselves on the To Do list and get the order right. Set your priorities. ME FIRST. MAKE SURE I AM HAPPY FIRST. Then you can give happiness to others around you, like your family. You are no good if you are depleted and empty.

Now if you are saying...

Me first? Really? I can't do that...

we are back to square one.

So let's get to the bottom of this sense of not being worthy of being on your own To Do list. Not worthy of being happy. Because that is the bottom line. That is the biggest insurmountable impediment for most of us... not believing we are worthy of those INSTEADs. Not one of us starts out as feeling unworthy. In fact, as children, we have the amazing egocentric piece to us that believes we deserve everything and deserve it NOW...

Think about your life... do you remember an instance when you started to feel unworthy? Does Jean's situation sound familiar?

Jean had a full life before her family expanded to include three cats, two dogs, one goldfish, a husband, one step-daughter and two sons. Then her life got *really* full. Having children and animals to take care of, plus working part-time, afforded her little free time. She felt bad about taking time for herself, even to use the pedicure gift card that her husband gave her! She needed help with feeling worthy again, since she lost it somewhere in the commotion of a large family and so many needy beings to care for.

Jean was actually annoyed with herself about her inability to make time for herself and felt bad about it. She just wanted to take some time without the guilt. Going through my Joy Course, surrounded with supportive women, gave her the necessary push in the right direction. Carving out the hour for the course once a week was a start. She realized everyone at home survived without her, and it began to get easier as she slowly put more time into her schedule for just her. Self-nourishment felt too good to give up.

Woman of a Thousand Excuses, Is That You?

Ah, yes the woman of a thousand excuses. The woman who has time to do everything but take the time to take care of herself. There is always something more important to do than take her own needs into consideration. **How are you going to be happy if you are busy giving yourself away all the time?**

How often do I hear how your kid has a sports game you can't miss, even though they have a game or practice every week? I can tell you that your kid's life won't be ruined if you miss one game. The errands, the chores—there's always an excuse for why you can't sit still and think about where you need to be in your life.

It is so easy to fill up your day and your world with all that is not urgent: errands, chores, mundane tasks that keep you from having fun and focusing on yourself. These tasks can get done if you use your time effectively! How you manage your time all goes back to your beliefs about whether you are worthy of living the good life. Having a family, big or small, will keep you busy, so plan ahead and plan well. The more busy you are with family tasks, the more effort you need to put into planning your fun time.

journal entry

You Are Worthy

When do I start feeling not worthy?

_____

_____

_____

Is it during a certain part of my day?

_____

_____

_____

Is it when I am having too much fun?

_____

_____

_____

Is it when I am being questioned by others about my decisions or actions?

_____

_____

_____

Is it when I am with a certain person or people?

_____

_____

_____

_____

Go deep, discover who you are and what sustains you. This does not happen overnight but is a journey over a lifetime. It is a journey worth embarking on; no one will know your self better than you.

> "I have heard enough warrior stories of heroic dancing. Tell me how you crumble when you hit the wall, the place you cannot go beyond by the strength of your own will. What carries you to the other side of that wall, to the fragile beauty of your own humanness?"
>
> —THE DANCE, ORIAH

Acknowledge the Pain

Have you taken the time to go to that painful place inside of your heart and soul? You know, the place in your being that makes you bend over and cry out loud? The painful memories that bring you to your knees and cry for God's blessing?

- » Have you been there? Are you able to go there?
- » Have you touched your own sorrow and felt the ache and the pain?
- » Do you lie next to your husband, lonely and tearful, silently knowing you have outgrown him?
- » Do you sit with thoughts of your mom, who passed away years ago, and cry tears of sorrow at how you still miss her every day?
- » Do you feel the ache of an estranged family member who holds an endless grudge and can't forgive, and has broken the family apart as a result?
- » Is your father unable to accept your lifestyle and choosing to stay away from you at all costs, forcing you to answer your children's most difficult questions about why their grandfather doesn't love them?
- » Do you feel the pain of your brother's drug addiction that brought him homelessness and jail sentences and how, in order to protect yourself, you can no longer answer his phone calls requesting cash?
- » Have you touched your own sorrow and felt the ache and the pain?

Stay there for a while. Don't rush the feeling away. Be there with yourself. It is okay. Don't grab the sleeping pills or the alcohol to make you forget. Feel it, work through it; you will emerge stronger. In order to get to that "feeling worthy" point in your life, you need to know yourself deeply.

We all have had events in our lives that were not joyful; some were tragic and some painful. Some happened as a result of our choices and others just happened. They were out of our control and left lasting effects. This can lead to lasting scars that whisper, "you are not worthy" or "you don't deserve to be happy."

My friend Lisa has a great story to share. I enjoy talking to her because she believes in true love and deep intimacy and never gave up hope that it would find her. When women spend time developing and growing, the hope is that their partner would also be doing the work so the connection is deep and intense. Ladies, you deserve someone who will not only treat you with love and respect but who can go to that deeper level of intimacy. Lisa had a tough childhood and spent most of her young adult years in counseling and deep prayer. She was single for most of that time as she did her best to focus on healing some deep wounds left by her family. As a result, Lisa has such depth and substance it is hard for her to tolerate being with people who are superficial.

She met John and she believes they are true soul mates. The intimacy and the comfort they have is beyond words. They can't describe it, but revel in the fact that they have it and it is so precious. It is a feeling most spend their days trying to find with their mate. Lisa is convinced they are so connected because John took the time to touch his own sorrow. Difficult family issues have plagued his life; the time he has spent in contemplation and letting it go has given him a depth that few people have. John doesn't spend time in self-pity that his life hasn't turned out how he had once hoped it would, but knowing that is also freeing to him. He now can work toward what he wants in his life, free of his past. The men Lisa had dated in the past were men who covered up their true feelings with defensiveness and surface stuff, never getting even close to the inner core. How do you have intimacy with someone who hasn't felt their own sorrow and emerged stronger and whole?

Self-worth is linked to that internal dialogue that is often reruns of our past. We replay the words of people who have told us we are not worthy or who have shown us little love and warmth. Their words play over and over in our minds. What has happened to us in the past has a direct link to how we feel about ourselves today.

Ladies, allow the therapeutic process to help you through any past unresolved issues. Many of us can't work through it and process it alone. It can be too painful, and opening up old wounds without proper guidance and support can land you in a very depressing place. You don't want to get there and not be able to get out of it. A therapist you trust can help you explore any issues you have and move you in the direction of a better, more worthy-feeling self!

Discover Your Strengths

What might you be good at? Are you working at a job now that lets you use your true gifts? In the wonderful book, *Authentic Happiness*, author Martin Seligman speaks to the concept of *signature strengths*. Everyone has something they are good at naturally. For me, it's speaking to and helping women; it comes naturally to me and fills me up with happiness. My day job at the hospital is challenging and I enjoy it. The part of my job that involves doing budgets and spreadsheets—well, I don't feel that's my strength or that it adds to my emotional well-being, but I have learned to do this over time. It's a different feeling when we use our natural strengths. We feel more content in life and more energized. **Joy comes to us when we are aligned with our purpose.**

When you are engaged in what comes naturally to you—whether it's teaching, nursing, or analyzing—you feel *good*. This good feeling adds to your confidence, your ability to stand tall and gain satisfaction from using your true talents. It might take some time to discover what these are, so don't rush the process; take your time in quiet reflection and be open to a process of trial and error. You may be surprised at what you are really good at when you try something new or something you have always been interested in! You may end up thinking *this* is what you were born to do!

By the same token, don't get discouraged when what you thought you were born to do doesn't quite pan out as planned. The point here is to find something you are good at—and do it. Some people go through life with no direction and no purpose. Do something in the direction of your dreams. Not sure what to do? Try one or more of these:

>> Talk to a career specialist.

>> Volunteer in a place where you think you might want to work.

>> Read up on the profession you are interested in.

>> Call your local state college and talk with a professor about courses of interest.

>> Talk with your close friends about your ideas, and keep talking until it shows up in your thoughts as an idea to go for!

>> Take a class online.

>> Believe you can do it.

>> Doing something instead of nothing will bring you one step closer to finding your true talents.

"Use your signature strengths every day to produce authentic happiness and abundant gratification."

–MARTIN SELIGMAN

YES! I believe Seligman's statement with all my heart! If you are working at a job where you are bored and not using your talents, I'll bet you feel annoyed, frustrated and depleted. This is the opposite of what you would feel if you felt your job is the exact fit for you, if you got excited every day going to work, doing what you love and believing you are good at it. You would carry with you a strong sense of purpose, knowing you are right where you need to be. What an amazing feeling!

journal entry

Strengths

What are your "signature strengths"?

Do you know what you are good at?

Are you working in a job now that allows you to use these strengths?

Have you had a past job that did?

How do you feel when you are using these strengths?

"I am worthy of receiving all the good life has to offer."

This is the mantra that should play over and over in your head.

I AM WORTHY.

Believe you are worthy of living the good life now, whatever that means to you. It can be yours, but it takes work and energy to move in the right direction.

Don't give up on happiness until a later date… want it now.

I have to warn you about something. If you start putting yourself first, I guarantee someone will get mad at you. Remember those people we met back in Chapter 6, the "it must be nice" people who are miserable and long not only to rain on your parade, but also to blast hurricane-force winds on your internal sense of worth? They will try to plant that seed of doubt, so you go back to that stance of "maybe I don't deserve to be this happy, maybe I don't deserve this whole day to myself. Maybe I should fill it up with errands like she does, or maybe I should go to all those school or church activities or work on my day off, take work home, etc."

Don't give in to the miserable ones!

The trick is not to second-guess yourself when you get the resentful looks from others when they learn about what you are doing or when you say "no" to them.

Ignore them. Set clear boundaries around what you are willing to do and what you are not. Don't let people project on you and take from your happiness.

Surround yourself with friends who believe they are worthy and are confident in their own ability to take time for themselves. Model yourself after them.

Be with those who encourage you to call in sick to go play. Be with those who can tell you are tired and need to slow down, not those who ask you to pick up the pace. Those who, when you tell them *you called in sick, went for a walk, saw a movie, went shopping, took yourself out to lunch, met a friend for coffee and then got take-out to bring home for dinner,* are excited for you and tell you:

YOU DESERVE A DAY LIKE THAT!

Value yourself, your time… YOU. Believe you are worthy of receiving all the excitement life has for you. I promise that once you get a taste of this beautiful, joyful life, whatever that means to you, you will want it more and feel even more worthy of receiving it all.

Put Yourself on the To Do List

It is possible to move from feeling unworthy to feeling worthy, as my client Rita learned to do. A mother of four small girls, Rita decided to stay home while her husband worked and provided the income. He never let his parenting duties interfere with his hobbies. An avid fisherman, he went away every weekend, sometimes on longer trips lasting up to ten days. Rita felt it is a wife's "duty" to be a martyr and not question her husband. She was tired, cranky and yelled way more than she ever thought she would as a parent. Her only night out was spent helping her aging mother, which brought no real enjoyment. She felt guilty going out to do anything else since her children depended on her for everything. She had no hobbies of her own, and rarely had time alone, even in the bathroom. She surrounded herself with women who are just like her—they didn't take risks, stayed with their kids with no breaks, and looked down on her if she made a move in her own direction. Being around other not-worthy women who didn't want to change was holding Rita back in her quest for internal happiness.

Rita decided to sign up for my Joy Coaching program and worked on her inner beliefs, those Martyr thoughts about what a mom "should" do. My advice to her, and to you if you're in a similar situation? Speak up and demand time for yourself. If he goes away, so should you. Your children need to watch you go out for "me" time, come back refreshed and capable of dealing with the flu or a night of not sleeping. Your children are watching you, taking in how you deal with your husband. They are being groomed for what they should expect in a future relationship.

As difficult as it was, Rita began to seek new experiences that would provide her with a new social network. It wasn't easy at first, but she talked with her husband, who was more than willing to help out, and secured Tuesday nights as her night "off." Then she started planning her free nights and life took on a whole new glow.

So this week, right now, put yourself on the To Do list. Give yourself a free night (or a few free hours or even fifteen minutes).

Let's imagine it's your free night… where would you go?

Here are some ideas, just for starters:

>> Go to a bookstore with a café and grab a cup of tea and read.

>> Go window-shopping.

>> Go to yoga or to a Zumba class.

>> Sign up for a class on something that's always intrigued you.

Commit to something that gets you out of the house for a certain day/night. You are more likely to make the time if you plan in advance rather than decide at the last minute. When you invest your money in something, you are more apt to go. And, scheduling the time away lets your husband or partner expect that you will be out.

Friendship

Your support group is important in this process of reclaiming yourself so you feel worthy of joy. Having supportive people around you can make all the difference. Your support group needs to consist of friends and family who support your growth and who encourage you to be true to yourself and don't make you feel guilty. When you're around inspired people, you become inspired to be your best. Take your cues from them. See how they move through life. Take a look at who surrounds you: How would you describe them?

Put Yourself on Top of the To Do List

Where are you on your own To Do list? In the Top 5?

What do you need to do to get up closer to the top? Like number 1?

Do you know what you want in your life?

What do you want?

Are you pulled by the "I shoulds"?

What are the top 5 "I shoulds" in your life?

I should

I should

I should

I should

I should

Now try incorporating what you've read in this chapter.

I should	but instead I will
I should	but instead I will
I should	but instead I will
I should	but instead I will
I should	but instead I will

Who would have thought that simply asking whether you are worthy can be a loaded topic? Let me tell you, you *are* worthy of all the good life has to offer you. If you don't believe it, people will treat you as if you are not worthy. Be gentle with yourself. Carve out that time for you, to be authentically you, to get in touch with your inner self and find that place where you began to feel not worthy. Let the past go, and if the scars run too deep and are too terrifying, seek therapy as a tool to freedom. Don't postpone this to a "better" time, because there will be no better time than right now.

Want the good life now. The amount of joy you feel will depend on how truly worthy you feel. Put yourself on your To Do list, and ask yourself, how can I make myself happy today? Without feeling worthy, you won't take risks; without taking risks you won't grow; and without growth there are no new experiences to allow you to feel joy, confidence and success. In the next chapter, we'll dive head-first into risk-taking and the benefits of feeling those butterflies and acting anyway.

CHAPTER 9

Risk to Grow: The Comfort Zone Dilemma

"And the day came when the risk to remain tight in a bud was more painful than the risk it took to blossom."
—ANAÏS NIN

. . . .

So far, we've talked about the obstacles that get in the way of creating and living the best life you can.

For many of us, it's the simple fact that we lost our dreams along the way, and forgot what makes us glow and feel passion.

For others, it's the idea that we don't deserve to take time for ourselves or live our dreams.

And for still others, there is a third reason we are not glowing, fulfilled and satisfied with a life well-lived…

I can sum it up in one word: CHANGE.

The discovery of what we need to do to be truly happy can be one we would prefer not to deal with. We think it might just be easier to keep living semi-happy because there is a huge risk associated with reaching for our deeper happiness, or finding our authentic self made whole.

The way we have been living? We thought it was working for us and then it stopped working. We no longer find comfort and joy in our ordinary days. So we have to make changes because we are worthy of being happy. (Go back and finish those Journal Exercises in Chapter 8 if you scoffed at the "worthy" word.)

You must make some active alterations to your life. There might be relationships to end, careers to terminate and start anew, homes to sell, and difficult conversations to have.

Now, I never said this was going to be an easy process, did I? A worthwhile one indeed, but for some of us, a not-so-easy one.

Oriah says in her book, *The Invitation*, "... *and sometimes I am afraid of my desires—afraid of what they will ask of me, what vision of myself or the world they will offer that may demand a sacrifice of my carefully cultivated way of seeing.*"

To reach your dreams, you will have to take some risks.

To experience a true sense of joy, you will have to take some risks.

That's another big word... RISK.

To make a change in your life, you will need to take some risks and break out of the comfort zone you have established. Are you ready?

"Start telling yourself that the smooth, comfortable life is not something to strive for, but rather a recipe for boredom and stagnation."
–WEST POINT PSYCHOLOGIST MICHAEL MATTHEWS, QUOTED IN *PSYCHOLOGY TODAY*, APRIL 2011

This chapter is especially meaningful to me because I am constantly pushing myself out of my comfort zone. Some say it is risky business, but I say growth is so important.

I know when movement is near, I feel it within me. I know when there needs to be a change in my life, whether it be career, relationship or simply a new direction awaiting me. I feel it. I embrace it; I can't run from it. It is both exciting and scary.

I remember when I left for Miami to attend graduate school. I had no intention of returning to the bitter-cold Northeast. I was a sun girl all the way. After three and a half years I felt the movement within me. It was time to head home. I fought it for a little while, thinking to myself that Florida was where I saw myself living for life. My inner voice said Fate had other plans for me, so who was I to fight it?

So I moved home, found a new apartment, a new job and new friends. Four months later I met my soul mate, who would soon become my husband. To backtrack for a moment, you should know that I had been praying for years to meet my soul mate, hoping I would soon see his face because I felt ready to settle down after continually dating with no luck and no real connection. If I hadn't taken the risk, listened to myself and moved, I would never have met my husband. This life I have, this most beautiful life with two amazing children, would never have happened.

In the long run, it is easier and more fulfilling when you follow your inner voice and go where you need to be rather than fight it. When you are resisting your true path due to fear or laziness, you are actually fighting against the tide, constantly struggling and never clear about where to go next.

I know people who have never in their life moved out of their comfort zone. Maybe they married a man they had been with forever, even though it wasn't great. It was all they knew. "He's a good man" or "We never fight." But does he make you truly happy?

Taking a risk would mean letting go of someone you know so well, dating, and feeling sad. Who wants to feel sad? Why not just stay where you are? You don't have to be sad if you stay, but do you feel really happy? Really excited about your love?

The relative brightness of your inner spark and glow reflects your choices in your life, and the degree to which you put yourself out there, open to new experiences, in search of true joy. **A joy that resonates within your soul and whispers to you, "you are in the right place, right here."** I have taken risks that resulted in feeling sad or hurt, but I would do it all over again if I had the chance. Why? Because I have learned something, or found my way to something better or more right for me.

If I try to ignore the movement within myself for change, I am continually reminded by signs all around me. You will feel them, too, if you stay tuned in to yourself. Some of us run at a fast pace and can pretend we don't feel it, or that we don't hear or read any of the signs we get. Some of us know it, and know we are being called into action by our own souls.

Here's the catch… leaving your comfort zone comes with risk. Any good move takes risk. I am in no way encouraging you to make a move you are not ready for or saying you should not be comfortable in your life where you are. My goal is to have you take a look at your life, career, partner, friends, hobbies and faith, and find an area in which you might need to push yourself a bit to grow. Sitting in quiet reflection can help you ponder whether it is time to move forward in some area of your life, and whether doing so requires taking a risk.

It's all about risk.

Do I stay or do I go?

Do I move forward? Or do I stay here? Maybe I should even take a step back. This is what I hear when I talk about risk. But "here" feels good. Comfortable, safe, and I can sleep at night.

But I've heard there is plenty more out there. Over there, in front of me, those steps forward are where dreams come true. *There* is where I grow.

So many of us get stuck here. We can think and dream in our safe comfort zones, but feeling the feelings associated with risk can be too overwhelming. Ask yourself these two very important questions:

1. Do you want to stay stuck?
2. Do you want to grow?

Do you want to stay comfortable and only imagine what it feels like to make your dreams come true? Or do you want to feel nervous and uncomfortable but achieve all your dreams? Here's what the process looked like for one of my clients.

Three years after her divorce, Alexa still wasn't dating. She felt her life was full with her two children and new business, and she didn't see how she could fit in a new relationship. Meeting someone felt scary and difficult, and every time we talked about it, her anxiety showed. Yet Alexa started preparations for a change in her life. She began working out, buying new clothes, slowly eliminating all the excuses she'd lined up about why she wasn't "putting herself out there." And then he just showed up! It was an old high school friend to whom she had reached out. Shocking them both, they fell in love. Now she's radiant with such happiness and passion!

In all my workshops, I weave in the concept of always growing. Staying stagnant leads to frustration, depression and isolation. There is so much to experience, so much to learn to keep our minds alert. Simple things like new classes at the gym, or a new church to discover, concerts to attend, adult learning classes to take, people to meet.

Take your job, for example—how long have you been there? Does it feel repetitive? Can you say "I can do this job in my sleep?" Do you really want to wake up in the morning and then sleep all day at your job? Do you enjoy being unable to use your critical thinking skills or other talents you have? What about learning a new skill or applying for a different position?

All actions come with risk. So many of us prefer to watch others take risks. Some might even talk about it and then when the time comes to actually act, they quietly retreat back to their comfort zone. *Not now*, you can hear them whisper, *not yet, maybe someday*.

I wish you the courage to take the risk to grow. Playing it safe in every aspect of your life does not allow for growth, for momentum, or for a strong sense of purpose.

I know why playing safe in the comfort zone occurs—it's safe! No other emotions go into this choice, just safety and comfort. Don't trade growth and personal fulfillment for safety. Risk comes with many different emotions; some are not tolerated well and the first hint of one of these may send you running for the comfort of your home. Stay with it my friends, it's your choice.

The Choice is Yours

Choices. Happy or sad. Good or bad. Go out or stay in. Ride your bike or go for a run. **Choices.** *Let life pass you by* or be called to action. *Watch your friends* enjoy their lives or be compelled to enjoy yours as well. *See those around you* take risks and grow or step out of your comfort zone and reap your own rewards. *Sit by idly and passion-less* or read some inspiring books and begin your soul-searching. **Choices.** *Watch your friends* discover love or be in search of your soul-mate and experience it for yourself. *Observe others* create and live their lives exactly how they want or go in pursuit of your lost dreams and create your own life. *Sit in the backseat* and be still or move forward and make it your time. It's your **choice.**

Standing by on the sidelines without being fully engaged in the game can leave you feeling bored and resentful. Stir up the passion. Fully participate in your life. Ignite your fire from the inside. Tap into your strengths, we all have them; what are yours?

Oriah states in her book *The Invitation: "I don't want to know how old you are. Your age tells me how long you have lasted, but not what you have made of the precious time you have been given. Lasting, enduring, is not enough. Tell me of the times you have taken a risk, and how you greet your fear."*

Choices. Give up or keep going. Be overwhelmed by an obstacle in your path or plow right through it. Cry and retreat, or cry and try again. **Choices.** By not making a choice you're still making a choice. It just might not be the right one.

Taking risks can feel like this	Taking risks can also feel like
nervous stomach	success
jittery	confidence
nail biting	boost to self-esteem
anxiety	excitement
sleepless nights	expanded horizons
uneasy	experience
challenging	GROWTH

Not taking risks feels
comfortable
stuck
smooth
easy

WHICH DO YOU PREFER?

RISK >> FEAR >> CONFIDENCE >> GROWTH

Having spent time thinking about risks and taking plenty of them myself, I came up with a way to describe the process that takes us from risk to growth.

Risk: Will this risk enhance your life in a positive way? Think about it. Seek guidance about it; talk with friends, family, mentors, anyone who can offer you a clear discussion of the risk involved. Do not ask your negative friends for input. When you are contemplating a risk that ultimately could make you a better person, don't spend time with someone who is going to talk you out of it. Don't go to them on purpose because when they tell you not to take the risk, you can wipe your brow and say to yourself, "Whew! I knew that was a bad idea!!"

To help you through the process, it's important to have a person whom I hope you already have in your life right now in some capacity, namely, a mentor. Do you have a mentor in your life?

A mentor can offer you the following:
Good advice.
Confidence to take the risk.
Trustworthy opinions in *your* best interest.
Knowledge.
Sound perspective.
Leadership by example.
Constructive criticism.

Mentors need to be:
Trustworthy.
Positive.
Unafraid to tell it like it really is, not how you want it to be.
Intelligent.
Humble.
Good leaders.

No matter where we are in life, we can all use a good, solid mentor. A professional mentor can walk you through the risk and help you envision probable outcomes. Some risks are not worth taking and can be detrimental to your life. If you are having trouble deciding whether the risk will have the benefits attached to it that you hope for, talk with your mentor about it. If your mentor is someone who has worked in the profession for years, she or he will have a wealth of knowledge to share.

Laura is a young attorney full of fire in her belly to make change. She is strong, smart and dedicated to the rights of children. There is so much to know about trial work, so much that is never taught in law school. She has found herself fumbling at times, making mistakes and losing self-confidence. She knows she needs guidance—her career depends on it. It would be a risk to ask, but the risk of not asking is greater. Laura asked an attorney she admired if she would be her mentor. Today, Laura feels completely different about her work. When questions come up, she stops by her mentor's office for a quick discussion. She feels more confident knowing she has someone who will steer her in the right direction and give her sound advice.

Mentors can help us keep the risk in perspective.

Fear: It's normal to feel fear, but move through it. If you stay too long in this step in the process, your fear can paralyze you and prevent you from moving forward. Fear is natural, but can be devastating to those who obsess in this stage. Fear can be overwhelming if you caught up in the "what if's?" What if it doesn't go right? What if this ruins my life? When you have people in your life who can be your cheerleaders and support you through and past this stage, you move on to the next step more easily.

Jan was excited about the possibility of a teaching job in China. She dreamed about it and was hoping she would get accepted. She was the first of her friends to contemplate making a move out of the high school where they taught and actually doing something more with her life. Her current teaching job was great, but she felt in need of a little change and excitement. She was very nervous, so before she accepted the position in China, she discussed it with friends who had never moved out of their own comfort zones. Not surprisingly, these friends gave her every reason why she should not go to China. Sickness, culture shock, her ailing mother might need her, too far away… All these "what if's" played right into Jan's fears until she became scared to death of leaving her present job. She declined the position and did not teach in China.

We are all fearful of taking a risk. Unless you really are immune to others' opinions, don't discuss your life with people who are negative and unwilling to make changes in their own lives. They certainly won't be happy to see you make changes in yours. If they can keep you low with them, they don't have to feel bad about the choices they did or did not make.

Confidence: Gain confidence, no matter what the outcome! The more you take steps out of your comfort zone, the more confident you become. Think of how you will feel when you go for several interviews. You'll gain interviewing practice, an increased awareness of what is required—all important information if you are going to get that dream job. If you never took the time to send your resume because of the risk and the fear, how could you walk into an interview with poise and grace and ACE IT? Confidence in yourself and your abilities will take you all the way, I can promise you that. Have the confidence to at least try!

Isn't that what we ask of our children?

I love to see parents who are active, well-rounded and willing to try new activities, foods and social groups. The best gift you can give your children is what you are showing them (which, by the way, has more merit to it than just telling them to do something and then doing the opposite).

Take part in the world, don't shrink back. There is so much out there to experience, don't be full of fear and afraid to take a risk. Don't sit on the sidelines of life and watch it pass you by.

Growth: Grow personally, professionally, emotionally and spiritually. As a strong, confident woman, you must be devoted to your own growth! There is no other way to grow but to expand your mind. Be dedicated to expansion in your life. Keep moving forward; this adds to your personal satisfaction and sense of purpose.

Remember the purpose of this book is to help keep you feeling joyful, whole, content and in love with your life. How can you do that if you haven't grown in years? How can you feel personally gratified in life if all you do all day is play it safe and watch others take the risk to grow? How can that smile have a true meaning of happiness if all you do is put everyone else on your to do list and not yourself? Take an active part in your life and LIVE IT FULLY. Challenge yourself in *all* areas of your life.

Diana is a 65-year-old retired teacher. She loves to learn, so she joined the local state college's "Explorer" program for retirees. Through the program, Diana can explore areas of interest and stay connected to others who also have a love of learning. This has led to fun gatherings and new friendships. At 65, Diana has an expanding social network and a strong sense of purpose from continued learning. Self-growth is a continuing process. Keep that mind stimulated!!

What Are Your Beliefs About Risk?

We often hesitate to take risks if we were not encouraged or supported to do so in our childhood. If we were humiliated for taking a risk that had a less than desirable outcome, we might tend to shy away from moving forward on something, especially fearful of shame, guilt and embarrassment. Let's take a look at family beliefs and how they influence our decision-making process.

Did your family encourage you to take risks throughout your life?

_____

Did you they support you when you tried new things?

_____

What if the result was not successful? How did they treat you? Were they still supportive?

_____

_____

Did you have role models to look up to? Who were they?

_____

_____

Did you often step out of your comfort zone as a child/adolescent/young adult?

_____

Why or why not?

_____

_____

Taking risks requires courage, confidence and passion. Fear can hold us back, consuming us to the point of feeling paralyzed. Following your dreams can be scary. Passion can give us that internal drive to step forward. We believe in something so deeply that we are ready to move forward, even with the risk of failure.

What if I fail? • *What if I succeed?* • *What happens now?* • *What will he/she think of me?*

These are questions that can play over and over in our minds. Yes, they are important questions to reflect on, but don't over-analyze them. Here is where your support group comes into play. Have people you can bounce ideas around with, friends who will love you no matter what the outcome is, family members who are just so happy you took the risk. Surrounding yourself with supportive people is especially important when you are deciding to take a risk in your life. We all need encouragement and a soft place to land in case it doesn't work out as we thought it would.

This is my favorite topic because I believe wholeheartedly that we need to keep growing as women. When I am in the company of women, I know instantly who has grown since high school and who has not. I can tell by the fears they hold onto, the drama in their lives and how little joy they experience as a result. I know women who have never left their comfort zone, EVER. Their level of joy reflects this choice. Those women who are strong, confident and ready to take risks continue to evolve as women. Not every risk will have the outcomes we wanted, but I encourage you to at least try.

I understand why taking a risk is not easy for many women. The feelings associated with risk are not comfortable, especially if you come from a family of non-risk-takers and you just plain don't care if you grow or not. Dedicate yourself to a life of confidence and joy, because you are worthy, remember? Your husband or partner should be your confidant, a best friend who is also your launch pad for new experiences and scary risks like that job interview downtown or signing up for that triathlon. Your husband can encourage or discourage you from taking a risk. We'll talk more about your partner's role in helping or hindering your joy in the next chapter.

CHAPTER 10

Husbands and Partners: Boosting Your Joy or Draining It?

"You are my soul mate, my love, my heart... now go away."
—JULIE McGRATH

....

When you finally meet the man of your dreams, the man you want to spend the rest of your life with, it is true bliss. Maybe you decided to have an engagement party and a nice wedding, you dreamed together on your honeymoon of starting a family, of what that will look like and how your life will be filled with love and joy. If you have a partner or a lifelong boyfriend with whom you have children, your partner can add to your joyful life or take from it. You are living in close quarters with someone whose positive, uplifting attitude, warm smile and comforting embrace can refresh even the most negative of days. They are who we need when we are elated or down in the dumps.

Our partners are meant to be our softer place to land, as we are for them. We can share everything and anything, knowing they will hold our feelings carefully and with love. When we spend our days with our soul mate, our days are brighter, we are happier and certainly more full of joy. It is proven that those in healthy, loving relationships live longer. Ah, life is good.

Take caution: as much as they can uplift you, husbands and partners can suck the joy out of you at an alarming rate. I have worked with many women who had to take a hard look at who was depressing them and holding them back from a joyful life, and some found it was their own partner. I don't say that lightly. When you recognize and acknowledge it, there is a deep sadness attached to the discovery. Once you know, it's hard to not know, which can sometimes mean change needs to happen. It feels like it is never a good time for this type of change. It can be heartbreaking with a big adjustment period.

I love to hear stories about dedicated husbands and fathers. The ones who sit for hours building Legos or who wear scrunchies on their wrists for their four-year-old's long hair. The man who's picking up a pizza with his kids in tow so his wife can have a night out.

I do believe the relationships we get into and how we act with men can stem from how we first experienced love from our fathers, whether we had a father present, whether he was a kind, loving man or an abusive jerk. (A book you may want to read is *Strong Fathers, Strong Daughters* by Meg Meeker.)

My father is an amazing man and I am forever grateful he knew how to parent correctly. His unlimited love and support for me allowed me to experience love with other men as healthy, nurturing and kind. I was lucky—not everyone has that.

Marriage is tough. Sometimes it even sucks. Throw in kids and it's anyone's guess how it is going to turn out.

So let's start there… marriage… tying yourself to another person for the rest of your life…

I remember when my husband and I first took Pre-Cana classes (the Catholic Church's version of "Intro to Marriage 101"). We had to do an activity outlining "what do you want to bring to this marriage that you had growing up, and what would you like to leave behind?" That was easy for me; I had a beautiful childhood and parents who loved each other. I truly was lucky and I am forever indebted to my parents for a life of their unwavering love and support.

However, no one told me *how* my parents did this. How they loved each other through all the ups and downs, through the sleepless nights and stressful days. I knew I was loved, but I wasn't taught how they dealt with it all. That's what they should teach you in pre-marriage classes, how to be married and be a parent.

Instead, you get married, have an amazing honeymoon filled with passion, love and dreams for the future. Homes, babies, careers and at some point, after the first or second child, it all changes. And not necessarily for the better.

You wake up, tend to the children and need to know every single detail of their schedule and your husband gets up, eats his breakfast and walks out the door to work. Hmm, interesting.

Do you know how many times I would yell, "I didn't sign up for this crap!" I meant every word. At the altar, I didn't say "I promise to love you and be your secretary, your maid, the children's maid, remember every detail about all of your lives and still try to maintain my career and my happiness." Whew! That's a lot!

My friend Todd Patkin, a motivational speaker and the author of *Finding Happiness*, once shared with me his thoughts on marriage vows. "I think it should say... I take thee to be my lawfully wedded husband/wife in sickness and in health so long as you continue to make me feel special and loved."

Yes! And I'd like to add "be my partner" in there somewhere.

The truth is, even with the best of husbands, we often get the short end of the stick. **Women hold up the world and that is that.**

My husband is an excellent father, "the modern father," according to my grandfather's girlfriend, who tells horror stories of her life tending to four children. Her husband would leave for work and she was left with no car, cloth diapers, no birth control and, I am guessing, plenty of resentment.

The modern-day father has a diaper bag slung over his shoulder, takes the children to the doctor's appointments, changes the diapers and snuggles with the children in bed.

There is a small percentage of men who are naturally this way. And no matter what kind of relationship you have with your in-laws, if you are married to a modern-day father, then send out some gratitude to his parents. They brought him up well and saved you a lot of work.

The rest of us have to train the fathers of our children.

Yes, I said "train." We need to:

>> Set the groundwork of expectations, and

>> Communicate constantly and every day about our needs.

If you think, "if only he would help more," re-think that. Try to communicate with him. Ask him to help out more, give him a chores list.

An ongoing frustration for me was my husband's blind eye toward the household chores. He would walk right past the overflowing laundry basket twenty times and not think the clothes in it might need to be washed.

How does anyone not recognize that?

Yes, it is quite maddening, but I will go way out on a limb here. He wasn't doing the laundry because I was. He never had to, so he never did. Would you do a menial task if someone else was already doing it for you?

If this all sounds familiar, I ask you… have you *asked* your husband to help?

Maybe you have had a different experience, but I have noticed that they will do it if you ask them to. They might not recognize that the laundry basket is overflowing or that there is not one more clean dish in the kitchen so it might be time to run the dishwasher. Instead of getting highly annoyed, why not *ask* him to do it?

I have found great results with these types of simple requests:

"Honey, can you run and empty the dishwasher?"

"Honey, it is your turn to make lunches for the next two nights."

Instead of getting annoyed, now I simply ask him to do something. I ask him to clean the dishes and vacuum. And guess what… he does.

I confess I wish he would actually do it on his own, but why let this bug me? I just remind him he has lunch-making duty this week.

Now, I know there's a percentage of women out there who struggle with equality of the sexes in the kitchen and household arena. I've witnessed a few myself. Some of you may say, "But he worked hard all day to provide for our family so why should I expect him to put away the socks?"

My answer?

You are a team, right?

I didn't get married to be the maid. Did you? Did you get married so you can do *all* the chores, take on the full responsibility of the children and, for some of us, work outside the home, too? Well, I didn't. At no point in those vows did he say, "I take you to be my lawfully wedded housecleaner..."

If your husband complains about helping out, remind him that carrying the full burden of the home, child-rearing and working is exhausting. Who would feel ready for passion after all that?

But more on that later...

If He Has a Life, Make Sure You Have One, Too

Before I got married, my husband, an avid snowmobiler, told me he was not giving that up. Perfect, I thought to myself, because I have a ton of hobbies and enjoy traveling alone, so this would work out fine. Honestly, for the most part, it has worked out. Each winter my husband goes away every other weekend and also for one week snowmobiling with his friends. I want him to have the time away, enjoying his friends and engaging in his passion. It makes him a better person. As much as my life has changed being married with children, I remind myself, so has his. Why would I not want him to enjoy time with his friends in a sport he loves?

Again, when we are full, complete women, we can appreciate the time he spends away and not feel neglected or rejected. If I am needy and codependent, I cannot do that easily; I will make him feel bad for leaving me. Everyone suffers.

I, in turn, go away as much as possible. I travel to the West Coast to attend professional training sessions, I go away local for scrapbooking weekends twice a year and visit friends in between. We all need our time away. I have met people who struggle for *any* time away at all. Here's an example.

My friend Carl is married with two small children. Before he was married, he was an avid hunter, and before the children came along, he took the time out to enjoy his favorite pastime. For Carl, who works very hard and takes his role of providing for his family very seriously, hunting gave him the break he needed to re-charge his batteries. When I recently asked him how his hunting seasons have been, he looked away and said he doesn't hunt anymore. When I probed further, he explained how his wife gets angry when he is leaving, even just for an overnight, so he would rather not do something he enjoys so he doesn't come home to a bitter attitude. He didn't think it was worth it.

My heart broke when I heard this. He told me his wife has no hobbies or interests, relies solely on him for entertainment, and refuses to get a babysitter to help when he is away. He has given up on his favorite thing to do. He shrugged and said, "That's okay, someday I will do it again."

Now how happy can Carl really be? How resentful might he be every time he looks at his wife? Does a woman really do this to the man she loves? Isn't that a breach of the marriage contract? I think it is. I wouldn't put up with that for a minute.

Get your own game. He goes away and you go away. It's about equality and having everyone happy and nourished.

As a side note, Carl signed his wife up for some of my events, and before too long she had renewed some of her old hobbies. Her passion for hiking allowed her time without her family so she could be "just herself," not a mom, not a wife. She looked forward to these all-day hikes with friends and eventually joined a hiking club. Now Carl can finally enjoy his hunting again without the sour attitude of a lonely, bored wife.

It takes work in a marriage for two people to get their needs met and to feel loved. It's about appreciation and dedication to being a better person, growing each year, not getting worse. Ladies, as much as I hear complaints about husbands, here is one complaint I hear often from men. Please read the following story with an open mind; the point is not about a woman's physical appearance, but about her spirit.

The following is from a friend of mine who agreed to share his story in his own words.

"I married her because we fell in love and I had never met such an amazing, smart, confident woman. I was and still am a good-looking guy, I take pride in looking good and I work hard. Years into our marriage, everything changed. The children came and

I accepted the fact that she would look different after having a few babies in her belly. She continued to gain weight, almost 70 pounds. I have continued to exercise, and try to motivate her to come to the gym with me, go for a bike ride or a long walk. She showed no interest. She would rather be with the children, and shows no interest in dressing nice or having sex. I know that deep down, she is very self-conscious about how she looks. I am no longer attracted to her. Once in a while I will catch a side-profile view of her, all fat, and my heart breaks."

"When we met she was beautiful, not super-slim but with a nice curvy body," my friend continued. "I can look past the weight, but this shows me she takes no pride in herself. When I attempt to touch her, she makes excuses and then always needs the lights off. There is no more passion. Nowhere in our vows did it say she could give up on her self and feel sad and sloppy. You see for me, it's not only that my wife gained weight, it's her whole mind-set. I try to talk with her, she gets defensive, telling me all I want is sex, which is not the truth at all. I want the wife I married, not the angry, self-defeating, heavy-set woman now before me."

I think it is so important that we work hard on ourselves, to get better with each day. I also hope your spouse or partner holds those values, too.

> "How to keep love fresh? The answer is the same as it is for any other activity. To be enjoyable, a relationship must become more complex. To become more complex, the partners must discover new potentialities in themselves and each other—so that they can learn what thoughts and feelings, what dreams reside in their partner's mind. This in itself is a never-ending process, a lifetime's task."
>
> –MIHALY CSIKSZENTMIHALYI, IN *FLOW*

Keep Love Fresh

Your relationship with your spouse will be tested in all ways once children enter the mix. There will be days when he is your hero and other days it feels like he's your enemy. Marriage takes work, communication and dedication to each other. After years of neglecting your relationship because you felt the kids needed more attention, you can't suddenly decide one day you are in a happy marriage. It takes the constant work of making sure each other's needs are getting met. Children can put a huge strain on even the best of marriages.

I get annoyed when I occasionally pick up a magazine in the waiting room of my dentist's office that shows headlines like:

"Get the spice back into your marriage, 10 hot sexy tips"

How about

"Don't let the spice out of your marriage in the first place."

After years of neglect, putting on a black nightie and sexy heels won't get you back on track. It might get him off, but where does that leave you?

Those magazine articles can make women feel bad, as if they are doing something wrong. Try not to lose that connection you felt when you got married. Take time to sit and talk. Dream about the future together. Find a hobby and stay involved with it when you have children. Make sure you have new experiences and let your spouse have his own adventures, and then sit together over coffee and share for hours. Give each other breathing room to grow and have friends and experiences with you and without you. That's how you keep the spice and the love alive.

"I felt upheld by the one dearest to my heart."
—LEIGH STANDLEY

When Times Get Rough

Marriage therapy offers a softer place to land if times get hard in your relationship.

There may come a point in your relationship with your spouse or partner when you just need some help. Both of you can't quite seem to figure it out and it is only creating more tension when you try. Maybe you need to separate or maybe you just need to have someone besides your spouse listen to you. Marriage therapy is a great place to start. Your medical insurance provider may be able to give you a list of therapists whose services they cover, or your primary care doctor or pediatrician might also have a list for you.

Psychologist Martha Bitsberger describes what you can expect in a therapy session with your spouse. You will learn how to negotiate, respect your partner's strengths and limitations, and gain some perspective on what is going on in your marriage. This is a safe space with a professional in the room, where you and your spouse can discuss feelings that might be otherwise too painful to talk about. Again, just like in individual therapy, you have someone validating how you are feeling and bearing witness to your story. That alone can be very powerful. Martha reports, "Couples counseling can bring a couple closer, helping them to feel more loving towards each other and more compassionate."

Husbands, partners, lovers—they can be a source of extreme joy or excruciating heartache. A source of joy on some days and joy suckers on other days. To find a true soul mate is a gift because that person will be the one loving and supporting you on your good days and your bad days. Being a family is a team effort that takes work and strong communication skills. It is well worth the effort to work toward a strong, successful team. One where you *both* are striving for individual and family goals and dreams. You *are* dreaming, right? You *do* set goals, right? I'll meet you in the next chapter just to be sure.

CHAPTER 11

Goals and Dreams: The Joy Essentials

"A dream is just a dream. A goal is a dream with a plan and a deadline."
—MY FORTUNE COOKIE

In this final chapter, I'll show you how to create your life exactly how you want it to be and set those goals and dreams in motion. "Create" means "to bring into existence." Creating is an action word, it's about the art of doing and moving. It is not a sitting-back-idle-waiting-for-something-to-happen word.

Again, coming from me, a working mother of two with one full-time job and my own business, I can tell you that it does take an enormous amount of effort to create your world exactly how you want it to be.

Isn't there something you have always wanted to do? You have it in the back of your mind and hope someday it will be brought to fruition. If not by you, then who? Are you still dreaming? So what's the problem? What stops us from making all our dreams come true? For starters, it involves a tremendous amount of effort. Whether you have one child or five, let's face it, you are tired after putting in the time to co-ordinate babysitters, your partner's schedule, your kid's dance class, a birthday party across town and your mom's birthday. What's left for us? Where is our time dedicated to making our dreams come true?

Creating the best life you can involves fighting for your own time. You are in the fight of your life! Go for it! Don't live a life of wondering "what if?" Can you imagine waking up in your late seventies wondering if you had just gone for your dreams, how different your life would be? How you always wanted to achieve a certain goal and now it's too late? You wish you weren't so fearful, or so dependent upon others. You wish you weren't so impressionable, so vulnerable to those negative people around you. You grew old with your story and your dreams still inside you.

If you have an attentive, supportive partner, you can overcome the time obstacle by offering an explanation, and some dates and times you will be out. You reassure him so he does buy into the idea that you taking time away will make you a happier woman, which in turn makes the whole household happy.

However, in other partnerships, it is like a well-rehearsed cross-examination from the prosecutor. **State your name, your reason for wanting a better, more joyful life, why, when, how much time needed, and then why again?** Ugh!

The mere thought of the possible argument that would ensue can make even the bravest at heart shy away. Who's got the energy for that?

Listen up, ladies—this is a crucial point. Back down or proceed forward. Tired and annoyed as you may be when you realize you married a person who has trouble uplifting you and making sure your dreams come true, you must move forward. It is a fight worth fighting. Continue to state your case, nicely and calmly. He will get it. Point out the reasons for doing what you are doing; show him the benefit to him and you will be met with a smile. If I take that extra course I could make more money, which will help with the bills. Or, if I get myself a personal trainer I will feel better about my body, and we can take the kids hiking, kayaking and skiing like you wanted. (If you throw sex in there somewhere you will get a nod of approval, I know, I hate to say it but it's true…)

I have sat with my head in my hands, tears streaming down my face, thinking it is easier to give in to the grind. There are weeks I don't make my kid read, I just sign his reading log anyway. I type his homework words for him and send him outside to rollerblade so I can sit and have a quiet cup of coffee. Bad mom, you think? You can think it. I am just honest. I find women who are like me, tired women who need a break and are honest about it. We laugh and I feel relieved. Homework sucks. Making dinner is an added stress. There are days when it is all just awful. The everyday routine of making lunches, doing laundry, cooking dinner, overseeing homework, handling baths and the bedtime routine. After many nights of reading stories and an occasional song, it goes something like this:

ME: Did you brush your teeth?

Kids: No.

ME: Did you get your pajamas on?

Kids: No, we are sleeping in our clothes.

ME: Perfect. Read yourself a book. Good night.

I know it's worth the fight for my time. It won't be offered to you. Don't wait for the red carpet and a limo ready to whisk you off to the spa for the day. Create those days. Find the energy within yourself. Your joy depends on it. Don't wait for friends. If they can't do it, don't let that hold you back. Go alone. So many of my experiences have been solo. If I had waited for a friend to come along, I would have never lived in Costa Rica or Honduras, attended amazing workshops in Arizona and California, joined a boot camp class, or attended scrapbook weekends.

Start the ball in motion. How do you see yourself in the future, where do you hope to be? Do you want to take the easy road, sit on the couch every night, give yourself totally to your children and then wake up one day when they are grown and feel empty, without purpose, wondering what to do next? Why not put your goals and dreams in action today? Is that possible? Yes, it is! Roadblocks and obstacles come with the territory. So expect them. That is where your level of resilience comes into play. When you are resilient and strong, obstacles won't become permanent roadblocks to achieving your dreams.

Very few people have someone in their life who asks intently, "Honey, what are your dreams? How can I help you make your dreams come true?" I hope you have someone like that beside you, but don't feel bad if you don't. That's why I am here, writing this book. I want you to have the life you always imagined. I am invested in women dreaming and setting goals for a more joyful life. Let the joy cup in your life overflow!

Await the words of the heart. What dreams have you put on the back burner? What do you wish for? What goals are you ready to pursue? Do you even know for sure which direction to go in?

Clear the chatter in your head. Be still. Be silent. The answers will be revealed if you are patient. It is time now to create the life you want. It takes courage to set your dreams in motion, determination to keep them on track, risk to take the first step, passion to fuel your inner fire, and joy in living the life created by you. And create it you must!

Get to know yourself, what is it that you really want in your life? Be still. Turn off the television, shut down your computer, put your phone on quiet mode for one solid moment. Think. Dream. Pray. Meditate. Give thanks. Ask to be led to where you need to be. There are signs all around you pointing you in the direction of your dreams. I truly believe nothing happens by chance. When you stay in tune with yourself and your surroundings, answers are everywhere. All around you are people you are meant to meet, places you need to go, but you must stay present to see them. Don't be three steps ahead of yourself. Be still. Pay attention. Be alert. Now is the time. Create your life exactly how you want it to be. Imagine a life of joy knowing you are living your dreams.

Let me share the story of what I call "the Lunch Transformation," when I had a lunch date with a dear friend who was in a place where she needed to change in order to recapture her joy.

And there I was, 37 years old, a loving and devoted wife, mother, daughter... and my world was rapidly falling apart. I have been working as a nurse for over seven years in a local hospital. I love my work. I enjoy the fast pace of being a Charge Nurse, I take control and do a great job. I sign up for committees and special projects throughout the hospital, all adding to the fulfillment of my work. Except for one small but HUGE problem: the Nurse Manager left and I could not apply for the position. I want that job. I know that job. Everyone knows I know that job. I only have an Associate's degree. I was overlooked on purpose; meeting with the heads of the hospital helped little. No higher degree meant no higher job. I could see myself in that job; I would embrace the challenge and thrive.

Instead, a less experienced man (who gave me a bad vibe from the beginning, by the way) was hired to run the department. He was stern, inexperienced and didn't like me. There were days I cried all the way home from work. My world, my favorite place to do 12-hour shifts, was turning into a depressing, frustrating place of employment. I tried, oh I tried to rally and be positive. I spoke with Human Resources, sought counsel from my colleagues, but in the end I would have to make some choices.

Change to overnight shifts and throw off my natural sleep balance? UGH!

Just work my normal hours and become cynical and nasty about how much I don't like even seeing his face? WORSE!

Request to change floors and leave my friends. NO WAY!

I met with my friend Julie for lunch. She is not just any friend. She is a positive problem-solver. I was distraught and tearful at the Cheesecake Factory restaurant, crying into my expensive salad. "What do I do?" I cried. My friend didn't skip a beat when she replied, "Go back to school and get your degree." Hmmm, yeah, I work full-time, have two small children and a husband, and my aging parents live with me. How would that even BE possible? She saw that I was thinking of the reasons not to, so she replied, "Go back to school, you have no choice but to advance yourself so you can become the Nurse Manager someday. You need a degree, go do it."

Well, yes, that did make sense. I am smart and could do it, but how do I put myself first? After years of worrying about my family, where do I come in on my to do list? How do I juggle the world and still get my needs met? Risk, it is taking a risk, and that feels uneasy with a side of fear. I learned about setting boundaries. It is hard to say no but I had no choice. School requires studying and homework and if I committed myself to school, I needed to matter.

My friend inspired this fire inside of me. There is a great quote from the article "Healthy Obsessions" (Psychology Today, May/June 2010) that says,

"If you intend to matter you must act as if you matter."

So I did.

The following day, I researched nursing programs and within a month I was signed up and ready to go. The day came that I went to orientation, scared and doubting myself. I drove to the coffee shop on the way, and there was my friend Julie in the drive-thru a few cars ahead. She didn't see me, but seeing her was all I needed to boost my confidence. I am going in the right direction and it feels great. My dreams are coming true. I am creating my world exactly how I want it to be.

KEEP DREAMING, set goals in all areas of your life. Keep moving forward.

Professional Goals

Once we get the job we love, we work hard at doing our best, learning all the new skills associated with the job, getting to know what is expected of us and meeting new co-workers. After mastering the skills, we then do it day after day and year after year.

It is so important to keep growing, and not let ourselves stagnate. When I hear "I can do this job in my sleep," it doesn't make me want to congratulate you. I feel sorry that you are not challenged in your work, and I know that soon you will be bored and burned out.

Burnout is not only for those out-of-control, chaotic, over-worked individuals. Mark Gorkin, author of *Practice Safe Stress*, uses this definition to describe burnout:

"Equally dangerous (as burnout) is chronic boredom and consistently feeling that you're underutilized or undervalued at work or lacking the opportunity to stretch your mind-body muscles in a meaningful way. Such a state gradually leads to smoldering anger, depression, or burnout just as out-of-control overwork does."

Acquiring new skills is so important. Training programs and workshops nearby and out of state (especially someplace really funky and cool), can bring learning and entertainment together in a perfect package. Some jobs actually reimburse you for learning new skills or offer advancement when you obtain new degrees.

When you are experiencing burnout, you are not a happy person. In fact, you are miserable. You hate your job, you feel like you are wasting your time, and it affects you mentally and physically. You are exhausted, have no energy and no enthusiasm.

Christina Maslach, in her book *Burnout: The Cost of Caring*, describes burnout this way: "People feel drained and used up." Basically, you have nothing left to give.

If you are in a state of burnout, it's time to look into a new profession, a new job and a breath of fresh air. Staying in a job where you are burned out will affect your entire life. You will be frustrated, cynical and hopeless. It will leak into your personal life. Going to a job every day that causes all those emotions makes for an unhappy person.

Remember that stress and burnout are two different things. If you have a stressful day or week, if you have good stress relievers, you feel better the next day. When you are in complete burnout, you do not wake up the next day not burned out. It is lasting, which is why it is so imperative to catch it before you are totally gone.

If you are not sure you are in full-fledged burnout, here's an exercise you can try. In the book *High-Octane Women*, Dr. Sherrie Bourg encourages women to take a weekend away, disconnecting from work completely. If you wake up the following Monday morning dreading your work shift, feeling anxious with stomach pains, you are burning out. She then encourages you to take two weeks off, disconnect from work totally and completely, and engage in all your favorite pastimes. If after these two weeks you wake on Monday morning dreading your shift, you, my friend, are in burnout.

If you are simply stressed, two weeks away doing what's fun will recharge your batteries and reenergize you for work. That is why vacations are so important. Saving up all your vacation and sick days and bragging about how you never take them doesn't impress me. In fact, it does the opposite. It tells me you have no balance in your life and you take little time to enjoy yourself. You are given benefits like time off for a reason, so use your benefits.

We all get those stress warning signs that tell us we could really use a day off from work to play. We could really use a mini-vacation or a long vacation. Don't give those days back to your employer unused! Take the days off to enjoy and play. Give yourself permission to play. In this economy, some can no longer afford vacations away with their families; however, a mini-vacation can be as simple as a day trip to the beach, the local park or to an amusement park. You don't have to drop $5,000 for a Disney vacation in order to make memories. Life can be simple, family-focused and fun. I know today we live in a complicated, busy world. But that means playtime is just as important, if not more so, for the reasons I just gave. The world is moving at warp speed; we're not slowing down to take a breath. With all the technology at our fingertips, connecting some of us to our work 24/7, it seems to move even faster. I don't care how much you love your job, we all need healthy breaks. If you give 110% all the time to your work and have no balance of play time, you are heading for burnout. Take care of yourself.

Remember to keep setting goals even if you are in the job of your dreams! You can be overworked or under-stimulated and find yourself so burned out you can't even muster up a small goal or new career dream. If you keep those goals always in your head, they can turn into the lifeboat you jump into when the time comes to move on.

Spiritual Goals

> "Be not afraid. I go before you always. Come follow me,
> and I will give you rest."
> –FROM THE HYMN "BE NOT AFRAID," BY ROBERT DUFFORD

What do I mean by setting goals in our spiritual lives? Spirituality brings peace and enrichment at the soul level. It adds to a most joyful and happy life. Seek a service, a religion, a belief that nourishes you on a deep level. Your spirit will feel renewed when you allow your higher power into your life. Don't shun God because you are feeling dismayed at a particular religious institution and its most recent set of scandals. Be in touch with God still, just try a new type of church. There are plenty to choose from. I had the privilege of being a keynote speaker at a women's retreat in Florida recently, where I joined women in their fifties, sixties and seventies. We shared an amazing weekend talking about joy, love and happiness. Some of these women have endured hardships throughout their lives: the deaths of children, spouses and friends; illness and natural disasters. I couldn't help but notice how their strong faith had kept them heading in the right direction, one of peace and strength. They held their faith dear and it certainly showed through in their smiles and their stories.

Spirituality should not be boring, punishing and obligatory. Whatever religious denomination or sacred space you choose, your worship service (or moments of deep reflection on and connection with something greater than yourself) should leave you with a feeling of love, peace and grace. I grew up Catholic, I made all my sacraments and saw the same unhappy people come to church every week, not seeming to get much from the services but only there out of obligation. Noticing that I was not getting much from the service, my mother tried another congregation. This church had—and still has—the music of angels. The singers gather and fill the church with such inspiration I am often moved to tears. I sing wildly and other times quietly, praying and being filled with strength.

Go when you feel you need it is what I recommend. Don't just show up every Sunday and wonder why you are even there. I enter the service, not every week, when I feel my soul calls for it, and I go for the music. Just because I don't agree with everything the Catholic Church stands for doesn't mean I can't go and be part of a service where I feel nourished. I have also worshiped in our non-Catholic churches. I bring my five-year-old daughter to a Unitarian Universalist church every once in a while when I feel the need to be in a different type of holy atmosphere. An added benefit of visiting the UU church is that my daughter can watch a woman minister deliver an inspiring message. A woman preaching inspiring news! Gotta love that!

My children attend Sunday school because I believe firmly that faith builds character. Whatever faith you choose to give your children is a true gift. Offering no faith and no belief is a disservice to your children. When a friend passed away years ago, he left two children ages seven and nine. He told me once, as he knew he was dying with months left to live, that he wished he had given his children faith, so they would feel comforted by thoughts of heaven and angels and the presence of God. Instead, their first introduction to any religious service was their father's funeral.

Find a service or a faith that nourishes your being. It might take work and many visits to different places until you find the right one. Keep trying. The right service, the right people can bring light into your life in remarkable ways. Don't settle for boring or obligatory, seek holiness! Seek to be full of grace! What I find troublesome in today's fast-paced, technology-savvy society is that there is less talk about God and more talk about the latest and greatest iPad or gadget. There's less focus on character and more on what some celebrity is wearing to an awards ceremony. Mothers, bring spirituality into your everyday life. Focus less on the superficial and more on the substantive way of life. Faith is a gift you give your children.

Personal Goals

What are your personal goals? To learn something new? Try a new hobby? Make some new friends? Expand your social circle? Do you need to say yes more often when you are invited to a girl's night out?

In my workshops, I spend a lot of time talking about how to say no and make time for yourself. However, I do realize that there are some of us who need a push to say yes, like the introverts who prefer a good book over dinner with friends or computer time over human time. There is a balance. You don't have to be the life of the party or go to events you don't enjoy, but being with the right people can be encouraging and refreshing. It is never too late to learn new skills, new languages or new hobbies.

Snowboard. Ski. Surf. Hang glide. Knit. Quilt. Speak French. Speak Spanish. Learn golf. Play tennis. Scrapbook. Paint. Write poetry. Collect stamps. Hike. Bike. Rollerblade. Design jewelry. Kayak. Learn outdoor wilderness skills.

Challenge yourself, ladies! Your inner joy will shine!

Physical Goals

Back at the beginning of this book, I reminded you that exercise is the number one stress reducer, not wine, not cheeseburgers, not sleeping pills. You don't have to have a gym membership to exercise. I'm talking about moving your body in any way you can that gets your heart racing. It can be dancing in the kitchen with your kids to Radio Disney, raking leaves, playing hopscotch or tossing the football around in the back yard, or hot wild sex that leaves you panting and close to a heart attack.

So what is your exercise routine? Do you have one?

Getting in shape is fun! (Or it should be.) There are a ton of different exercise classes and gyms for just women, and you can find personal trainers in nearly every city and town. Involve your family in the exercise routine and develop a healthy tradition of bike rides, hikes and walks on the beach.

It's easy and just takes the first step.

Now here are the tough questions…

Are you happy with how you look? Are you able to dance wildly around your bedroom in your bra and undies? Or are you all covered up, shy at how much weight you have gained being a mother?

Feeling good about ourselves does not mean we have to look like the Victoria's Secret models or fit into skinny jeans. (Those super-skinny jeans are better suited to teenagers, anyway—remember the fashion rule that says if you wore a look the first time it was popular, it's probably not appropriate for you when it returns 20 or 30 years later?) Don't waste your time on chronic dieting. Focus on being healthy and believing you look good. My friend and colleague Andrea Cohen, a food psychology coach, says, "There is a powerful cultural pressure pushing women to strive towards indefinable and unreachable goals of beauty and perfection."

Chronic dieting, according to Andrea, causes the following:

>> Nutrient deficiencies

>> Digestive issues

>> Mood swings

>> Fatigue

>> Binge eating

>> Imbalanced hormones, especially insulin and cortisol

>> Weight gain

If you are in good shape and feel good physically, why waste energy concerned about how your body looks?

My friend Claire is beautiful. Her body is curvy and gorgeous; she exercises and eats right. Yet, she has low self-esteem and constantly compares herself to other women she believes are in better shape. More exercise classes at the gym will not raise her self-esteem. Be careful of spending too much energy in the wrong place.

If you spend much of your time focused on keeping your body in good shape, balance that with keeping your mind in good shape. Devote just as much time to making yourself a better person as to fitting into that size 8 dress.

Curves are beautiful. It took me years to realize that curves are wonderful! Celebrate your body! Take good care of it by eating right. If you have trouble doing this, don't just go for the latest fad diet. Instead, consider trying programs like Weight Watchers or a counseling session with a nutritionist to develop good eating habits. Andrea works with women who want to change their relationship with food, and, lucky for me, she also lectures at my events for women. Andrea offers these simple rules about eating:

>> Slow down when you eat

>> Don't eat when you are stressed

>> Be nice (to *yourself*)

>> Stay aware (mindful eating = mindful living)

Feeling good in your body is a wonderful feeling. It is also a freeing feeling when you can say,

"Yeah I look good. My clothes fit just right. This outfit is perfect on me."

Kristin had a beautiful body in high school; she was a cheerleader and voted the prettiest girl in school. She never had to watch what she ate and she exercised, but not intensely. After having two children, her body changed. She could no longer eat what she wanted and she gained 40 pounds and felt horrible. Her self-esteem plummeted and her wardrobe consisted of sweat pants and baggy shirts. She longed for a better body, and she would frequently post her high school pictures on Facebook instead of recent ones because she was too embarrassed. With encouragement from her husband, she learned in a group setting how to eat healthy. In no time she was losing the weight, each week setting goals for herself and feeling elated. After five months she was exactly where she needed to be. She went on to lead a group, encouraging other women that it is possible to set goals and reach them.

The pressures on women to look a certain way come from many directions. I just noticed that all the Barbie and princess pictures my daughter prints from the computer are tall blonde girls with large breasts and long skinny legs. What is that telling my brown-haired beauty of a daughter?

Enough with these foolish stereotypes of women! Enough!

Love your body now, even if it needs work. Love yourself first!

Good, achievable goal-setting is in the details! When we are determined and driven to reach a goal, the little steps are the most important ones.

journal entry

Goal Setting

When was the last time you set a goal?

What was it?

journal entry

Goal Setting (continued)

Did you achieve it? If not, what happened?

_____

_____

_____

Did you share your goal with someone? Who? Why did you pick this person?

_____

_____

Did you encounter any obstacles in achieving your goal? If yes, what were they?

_____

_____

Did the obstacles prevent you from reaching your goal?

_____

Are you a dreamer? Do your dreams turn into realistic goals?

_____

My wildest dream is...

_____

_____

What is something that keeps you from reaching your goals?

_____

_____

Was there a time when you thought you had a perfect Plan A and then realized it was not going to happen as you had hoped? Were you able to come up with a Plan B or Plan C?

_____

_____

Fear of taking a risk can be a big obstacle for many people, as we discussed in the previous chapter. Going after your goals and dreams is a risk that can feel scary. It requires hard work, realistic expectations, courage and perseverance.

What has helped me as a parent is to always have a Plan B in my back pocket. There are times when events don't happen as planned and children get very upset. I allow them to sit with their feeling of disappointment and afterward we process it together. I encourage them to come up with a Plan B and keep going.

One of my favorite books for lighting a fire in your life is *Brainstorm: Harnessing the Power of Productive Obsessions*. In it, Eric and Ann Maisel explain the power of "healthy obsessing" to get your goals accomplished, to ignite an amazing idea, and to see it through to fruition. It's about finding something you are excited about and allowing the floodgates to open. Doesn't that sound wonderful, amazing and fantastic? Below, I'd like to share some of my favorite lines from this book. Related to coming up with an idea (productive obsession), the Maisels say, "Get it named—and get ready to let it invade you."

Focus your time and energy on your ideas and goals, not just half-heartedly but whole-heartedly and fully. Choose an idea that will get your adrenaline pumping, that will excite and thrill and challenge you. What goal do you want to accomplish? If it is to run a marathon, get excited about it, research the best running shoes and *buy them*, get on a running program *and RUN*. Wake each day excited to fulfill this goal. According to the Maisels, in a *Psychology Today* article (May/June 2010), when you engage in "healthy obsession" you are really:

Learning how to extinguish distractions so that you can concentrate, and

Retraining your brain, asking it to halt its pursuit of fluff and worry, and to instead embrace its own potential.

Seek to be ignited not defused. Don't be the woman saying, "Well, I really want to run a marathon but, oh well, maybe tomorrow I will start to look into it," or "I can't seem to get motivated." I often see women with many broken goals and dreams because they just can't seem to follow through. They have been meaning to join a gym or take an academic class to further their careers, but just can't get there to do it. Does Margaret's story sound painfully familiar?

Margaret is a stay-at-home mother who happily gave up her career when the kids arrived and stayed home. Over the years, she has lost her purpose and continues to stay home despite both kids now being in school. She takes on the entire burden of the household, a situation for which she unfortunately set the tone when she decided to stay home, not knowing it would become just that, a burden. Her husband happily goes to work each day, never taking a moment to broach the subject of his wife's dreams and goals. It never occurs to him to take a moment to start the conversation. She doesn't bring it up, her self-esteem is at a low point. He occasionally makes comments about her getting a job, because she never has any extra money to do fun things and she feels stuck. She is a smart woman with smart friends who encourage her to get moving, and offer to help her and guide her. She knows she needs to do something but never can get to a point of actually figuring it out. It is easier to just turn on the television and fill her mind with useless chatter. Her friends have stopped asking her what's going on, so now it is up to her to make the changes. It's been two years and there's still no movement in her life. Her happiness level reflects those choices. Are you a Margaret?

> "If you keep your thinking as small as possible, you will probably feel and act small."
>
> –ERIC AND ANN MAISEL, *BRAINSTORM: HARNESSING THE POWER OF PRODUCTIVE OBSESSIONS*

Yup, that's about right.

Ladies, this is your time! Get moving in the right direction! It takes work, but the payoff is extremely psychologically lucrative. You can't afford not to. Your happiness and joy are at stake. Create your life exactly how you want it to be.

>> Celebrate even the smallest of accomplishments.

>> You signed up for a course! Make cupcakes and celebrate.

>> You lost five pounds! Go for a family hike!

>> You graduated from college! Plan a weekend away.

>> You completed a task that required you to step way outside of your comfort zone! Call a friend and get your nails done.

Celebrating is a happy, joyous thing to do—especially when you include the whole family. Your children watch you as you experience that successful feeling and they take notice. They believe they can do that as well. Include joy in your life as much as possible. There are just as many reasons to celebrate as to not. I realize your world is not happy all the time, there is pain, strife and sadness. Why not take the time to celebrate the good?

The Maisels recommend that we "forget about guarantees: opt for commitment." Many of us want to know it is going to work out perfectly and as we imagined before we make any type of movement in our lives. It can be scary to make a move, especially if you have stood still for so long. It is easy to hear "Go for your dreams! Go for your goals!" These things are easy statements, hard tasks. To ease your way, surround yourself with people who want to see you succeed! People who want to celebrate even the smallest of accomplishments. You need to do the hard work of putting all the building blocks of resilience into place so that you have the courage and the tenacity to go full steam ahead in the direction of your dreams. Open a bakery. Go back to school. Write a book. None of these have guarantees attached. What can be guaranteed is that in the process you will grow in ways you never imagined. A strong, healthy, confident, joy-filled woman will emerge.

To conclude, let me recap the highlights of this plan for you to reclaim your joy.

1. Stop that vicious cycle of blah. Only you have the power and hopefully the drive to kick-start your life in another, more satisfying direction.

2. This path to reclaiming your joy involves growth, expansion and risks, so be prepared. The journey back to joy is not always easy or comfortable, but the rewards of feeling completely nourished and self-confident will be well worth it.

3. Surrounding yourself with good friends who really know you can prevent a stress disaster waiting to happen. True friends care for us and genuinely look out for our best interests.
4. It is your responsibility to build resilience in your children.
5. It is important to distinguish what is important to you and what is not. What events and places bring you joy and which ones take from it?
6. Don't postpone happiness until a later date... want it now.
7. Let go of guilt and believe you are worthy of joy.
8. Face your fears and take the risk!
9. Enlist the help of your spouse/partner to get household chores done, make dinner, and have passionate sex on a regular basis. Communication is the key to success!
10. Know what your dreams are, set goals, and make them happen to create the joyful life you want.

I want you to find the joy in your life, I feel it is my purpose in life to help you actually find joy and live it every day. I enjoy watching once-tired, worn-out women become empowered and confident. Once you get the feeling of inner strength that comes from setting your personal boundaries and carving out time to refresh your spirit, you will never go back to your earlier self. I promise you that. The feeling will be too great, too pleasurable to return to being a mother who only does for others.

You're a mother who sacrifices on a daily basis. I know you put your children before yourself in so many ways, and I applaud you for dedicating yourself to being the best mother possible. Such love and dedication means constantly giving of yourself to everyone around you, but it can deplete even the finest of mothers. Nurturing yourself and finding time to play is not a luxury, but a necessity, if you want to live a joyful life.

Restoring your spirit through setting your personal boundaries and creating more time for you will go a long way. I want you to glow, to radiate joy! All of the goal-setting, the communication and the dedication to self takes work! To actually find a balance between work, family and free time takes effort and planning, but as you have seen in the stories in this book, it is work worth doing.

I hope after reading and digesting all the information in this book that you have decided to put yourself on the top of your own priority list. Fit yourself in to the top five of your "to do list" every day to remind yourself to take the time to have fun, nourish your soul and slow your world down a bit. Take a break from mommy land; as beautiful and rewarding as it can be, it can suck the joy out of you at an alarming rate. So can the people you hang around with. Take a social inventory of those closest to you and make any necessary changes now. Be with those who support and uplift you. Your personal journey to joy depends on it. When you are radiating happiness, your children feel it and can rejoice in it also.

It is all up to you how much effort you put into having a fabulous life. Having a joy-filled, fulfilling life takes work and takes making the right choices about how you spend your time and who you spend it with, and knowing when it's the right time to take the risk to grow. Life is a journey, with growing, learning, and becoming better as each day passes. Make that commitment to yourself. Be joyful now. Today is a new day, make it the day you decide you are deserving and worthy of living an exciting, passionate life. I wish you courage and many blessings on your journey. Jump for Joy! You are amazing!

How Wonderful the Feeling of a Strong, Confident Woman

How wonderful the feeling of a woman who is full, who is content, who feels worthy and who makes the right choices.

How wonderful the feeling of a woman who makes the right decisions, who believes in her strengths, her capabilities and doesn't spend much time trying to correct her weaknesses.

How wonderful the feeling of a woman who capitalizes on her strengths, who doesn't let the past define her, who doesn't try to be better than anyone else in her life.

How wonderful the feeling of a woman who is creating her life exactly how she wants it to be, a woman who sets boundaries for herself, who can disappoint another to be true to her self.

How wonderful the feeling of a woman who knows the feeling of going from lack to abundance, a strong, confident woman who has the feeling of contentment with her self.

How wonderful the feeling of a woman who is fully aware and insightful, spending time in quiet reflection on how far she's come and where she hopes to be.

How wonderful the feeling of a woman who sets goals and dreams for herself, always looking forward, reaching, not dwelling on the past, only looking back long enough to know she never wants to return there.

Being better than you used to be requires not dwelling in the past but reflecting long enough to marvel at how much you've grown.

Being better than you used to be is about making positive choices each and every day.

Choices that affect your happiness, nourish your being and bring you joy.

Being better than you used to be is about igniting your spirit in such a way that you feel fully alive and vibrant.

Be This Woman. Be Better Than You Used To Be.

Listen to your inner voice.

This is your life, live it well.

What does your inner voice tell you?

Dump the man and start dating, be in search of your soul mate.

Where does your spirit need replenishing?

Go to France for a week and learn the language.

Do something so out of the ordinary that your friends say "*Wow*, I wish I could do that."

Take your kids on an adventure picnic.

Book a night at the spa with your friends and pamper yourselves *silly*.

Not what society or your family tells you is "right," what feels right to you?

Kayak with your best friends every Saturday morning, that might feel right.

Plan your dream vacation.

Learn to play the guitar at age 50.

That feels right.

Sing as loud as possible whenever possible.

Say *YES* to you every day.

References and Resources

References and Further Reading

20 Years Younger: Look Younger, Feel Younger, Be Younger! Bob Greene (Little, Brown and Company, 2012).

Authentic Happiness, Martin E.P. Seligman (Free Press, 2002).

Brainstorm: Harnessing the Power of Productive Obsessions, Eric Maisel and Ann Maisel (New World Library 2012).

Burnout: The Cost of Caring, Christina Maslach (ISHK, 2003).

Finding Happiness, Todd Patkin (Step Wise Press, 2011).

Flow, Mihaly Csikszentmihalyi (Harper Perennial, 1990).

Happiness: Unlocking the Mysteries of Psychological Wealth, Ed Diener and Robert Biswas-Diener (Wiley-Blackwell, 2008).

High Octane Women, Dr. Sherrie Bourg Carter (Prometheus Books, 2011).

The Inner Game of Stress, W. Timothy Gallwey (Random House, 2009).

Intimacy and Solitude: Balance, Closeness and Independence, Stephanie Dowrick (W.W. Norton & Company, 1996)

The Invitation, Oriah Mountain Dreamer (Harper San Francisco, 1999).

"Practice Safe Stress," Mark Gorkin, LICSW (2004)

The Psychology of Happiness, Michael Argyle (Routledge, 1987).

Something More: Excavating Your Authentic Self, Sarah Ban Breathnach (Warner Books, 1998).

"The Tough Track," Jeff Wise. *Psychology Today*, April 2011.

Resources—Where to Get Help

Martha Bitsberger, Ph.D., Psychologist
marthabitsberger@gmail.com

Andrea Cohen, M.Ed., Certified Food
Psychology Coach
www.fullcirclefoodcoaching.com

Michelle Gallant, LCMT, Therapeutic Body
Work and Yoga
mchgall@comcast.net

Leigh Sabroe, The Kid Chronicles
Facebook page
www.facebook.com/#!/pages/The-Kid-Chron-
icles/125883827516097

Where's the fu*#king mommy manual?
www.facebook.com/
wheresthefckingmommymanual
www.wheresthefckingmommymanual.
wordpress.com

National Alcoholism and Substance Abuse
Information Center
1-800-784-6776
www.addictioncareoptions.com

National Suicide Prevention Lifeline
1-800-273-8255
www.suicidepreventionlifeline.org

Alcoholics Anonymous
1-800-327-5050
www.aa.org

National Alliance on Mental Illness (NAMI)
1-800-950-NAMI (6264)
www.nami.org

National Eating Disorders Association
1-800-931-2237
www.nationaleatingdisorders.org/
get-help-today/

National Domestic Violence Hotline
1-800-799-7233
www.thehotline.org

ABOUT THE AUTHOR

A LICENSED SOCIAL WORKER, Julie McGrath watched women disappear into parenting, relationships and work, losing their true selves and desires in the process. The women around her were becoming empty shells of who they once were, full of guilt at the prospect of taking the precious time they needed for themselves. A strong advocate for women, Julie said, "Enough!" In 2009, she created The Joy Source to encourage and empower women to rediscover themselves, find their joy and passion, and then live it! Through The Joy Source, Julie leads groups and getaway weekends for women, offers individual joy coaching in person or by phone, and publishes a free, online magazine, The Joy Ride (subscribe at www.thejoysource.com).

For the past eight years, Julie has worked full time as the Director of the Psychiatric Crisis Team in a hospital emergency room north of Boston. Along with her husband Kevin, and her two children, Jared and Jill, she lives on Boston's North Shore and finds joy in sunny summer days, scrapbooking and being in the company of good friends.

For more inspiration and information, visit www.thejoysource.com or follow The Joy Source on Facebook.

Contact Julie at julie@thejoysource.com or 978-854-6935.

You are joy-worthy!

Made in the USA
Lexington, KY
10 November 2012